PENGUIN AFRICAN LIBRARY AP14
Edited by Ronald Segal

The New States of West Africa

KEN POST

KEN POST

The New States of West Africa

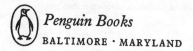

Penguin Books

BALTIMORE · MARYLAND

Penguin Books Ltd, Harmondsworth, Middlesex, England
Penguin Books Inc., 3300 Clipper Mill Road, Baltimore 11, Md, U.S.A.
Penguin Books Pty Ltd, Ringwood, Victoria, Australia

First published by Penguin Books 1964

Copyright © Ken Post, 1964

Made and printed in Great Britain by C. Nicholls & Company Ltd
Set in Monotype Plantin

Maps drawn by N. S. Hyslop

To my colleagues and pupils at Ibadan

Contents

Foreword and Acknowledgements

This book grew originally out of a course of lectures on *The Political Systems of West Africa*, given by me at the University of Ibadan in 1962–3. In assessing the material available while preparing these lectures I came to the conclusion that an attempt should be made to establish a preliminary set of generalizations about the sociological, political, institutional, and economic situations in which the new states of West Africa find themselves, and in doing so to consider French-speaking and English-speaking West Africa together. This, rushing in where angels would no doubt fear to tread, is what I have tried to do here.

The following chapters are based, therefore, upon as wide a reading of documentary and secondary material as has been possible, together with visits to nearly all the relevant countries in the course of the last five years. In a book of this length detailed references are impossible, but the books, articles, and government publications which I have found most useful appear in the bibliographies. These have been attached to individual chapters, to enable the reader interested in a particular idea to pursue it further. Statistics used have normally been drawn either from the publications listed or else from the digests of statistics which various governments publish periodically. It is difficult to guarantee a high standard of accuracy in every case. All translations from the French are my own, except where otherwise indicated.

'West Africa' has been taken here to include the countries from Mauritania to Cameroun inclusive. The inclusion of the latter may give rise to comment, since before independence it was administered with French Equatorial Africa, the territories of which are not included. It is to be hoped that the intrinsic interest of Cameroun as the scene of a major rebellion in the last years of colonial rule, and because of the federation of French- and English-speaking territories to constitute its final form, will justify its inclusion. The French spelling of this name has been used in order to distinguish it from the British Northern and Southern Cameroons in the period 1919–61. Similarly, the French spelling 'Soudan' has been used where necessary to refer to the present Mali, in order to distinguish it from the former Anglo–Egyptian Sudan.

The word 'territory' has been used to describe a given geographical area when it was under colonial rule, and 'country' to describe it after independence; this, it may be hoped, will avoid confusion caused by the duality of 'Colony' and 'Protectorate'. 'State' has been given a capital letter when it refers to 'the State' in the sense in which that term would be used in political philosophy. With a small letter it is used to refer to the newly sovereign entities which are the object of our attention. Similarly, 'Power' refers variously to the leading countries of the world, while 'power' is that vital abstraction, possession of which forms so much of the stuff of politics.

I owe much to the comments and criticism of others. Dr Archibald Callaway, Billie J. Dudley, Dr William J. Hanna, Dr Gerald K. Helleiner, George Jenkins, John P. Mackintosh, Charles J. Patterson, and Dr Sayre P. Schatz have read parts of this book and saved me from many abuses of fact, logic, and style. Any errors or absurdities which remain are entirely my own responsibility. I also had the great advantage of discussing this book with Thomas Hodgkin while it was still in the planning stage, though it has changed shape considerably since then.

As always, the labour of others on my behalf has been great. In particular Mrs Valerie Bloomfield and her staff in the library of the Institute of Commonwealth Studies of London University helped me greatly with printed material. Mrs Anne Mobbs typed most of the first draft, and my mother part of the first and the whole of the second draft. Merely to express my gratitude seems inadequate recompense for their pains.

University of California   K. W. J. POST
23 September 1963

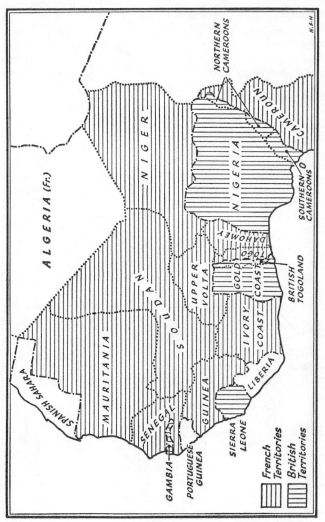

Map 1
West Africa in 1952

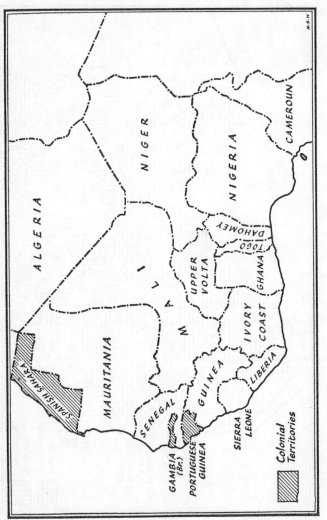

Map 2
West Africa in 1962

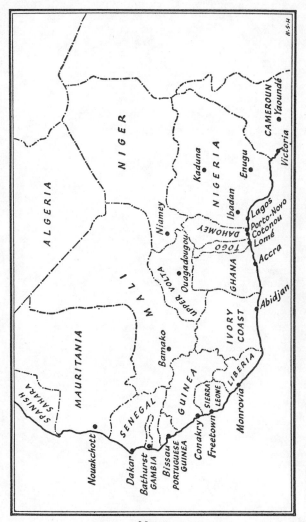

Map 3
Important Towns in West Africa

1 The Path to Independence

In the space of fifteen years after the end of the Second World War, almost the whole of West Africa ceased to be the colonial possession of one or other European Power and became a patchwork of politically independent states. This change was the work of the modern nationalist movements, and the studies of scholars in the last few years have enabled us to see quite clearly the way in which these movements developed in reaction to the colonial situation.[1]

The colonial situation itself was in its final form the result of the decision of France, Germany, and Britain to commit themselves fully to imperial expansion in Africa from 1884 onwards. The bargaining and treaty-making of the next two decades left France with the lion's share of West Africa in terms of area – some 1,604,000 square miles, compared with Britain's 497,000 – but in terms of potential riches British West Africa's 25,000,000 people offered far better prospects than French West Africa's 14,000,000.[2] Moreover, France's eight territories (seven from 1932 to 1947, during which time Upper Volta was divided between her neighbours) included large areas of desert or semi-desert, with Mauritania, Soudan, and Niger including the western and southern parts of the Sahara. One state of course already existed in West Africa when the Powers began their imperial expansion. Liberia, founded as a colony of freed slaves from the U.S.A. in 1847, has enjoyed political independence since that date. Germany for its part did not remain long upon the scene. Its imperial rule over Togo and Kamerun ended with the First World War, when part of the price of its defeat was the loss of these possessions to the victors, Britain and France, who divided them up to give the larger share in each case to France. The resultant four new territories, however, were not to be the unqualified possessions of these Powers. Instead they were mandated territories of the League of Nations, and after the Second World War trusteeship territories of its successor, the United Nations Organization. This was to be of great significance for their future evolution towards independence, but it did not in fact save them from the basic features of the colonial system. For although the systems which Britain and France set up differed considerably in matters of detail, and indeed in the assumptions behind them, they had important basic features in common.

First of all, colonial rule in West Africa, like colonial rule everywhere else, represented the dominance of a privileged minority, and one moreover which was immediately distinguishable by the colour of its skin. In this respect all Europeans were the same, whether they were agents of trading companies, administrative officers, or missionaries. However much individuals differed, all Europeans were necessarily treated with more than usual deference, and the consequences of offending any one of them were more than usually severe. Secondly, in the last resolve and sometimes with little attempt at disguise, the rule of this minority had been established – and was inevitably sustained – by force. Thirdly, it was the actions of this minority, indeed its very presence, that in fact set in train the series of social changes which was to give birth to nationalist movements and bring the colonial systems themselves to an end.

These social changes will be discussed in more detail in the following chapter. Suffice it to say here that one of their earliest effects, in both British and French West Africa, was to create a group of men who were able to perceive what they considered to be their rights, and to ask for them. In British West Africa from the last decade of the nineteenth century onwards there sprouted and flourished at various times organizations like the Aborigines' Rights Protection Society or the National Congress of British West Africa. Moreover, while these might be limited to the coastal towns and were controlled by the richer and more highly educated, the ideas originated by them and the arguments they advanced were taken up and discussed in the innumerable debating societies, local improvement unions, old-boys' associations, and mutual-aid societies which were to be found wherever there was a concentration of the literate. In French West Africa the picture was rather different. Tighter control by the French over the activities of their subjects (and, perhaps even more important, the existence of far fewer educated men) meant that bodies like the National Congress did not develop. Organized politics were confined to the citizens in the four communes of Senegal (Saint Louis, Gorée, Rufisque, and Dakar), which between 1848 and 1852, and then continuously from 1872, sent a deputy to the National Assembly in Paris. This lone representative could exert little pressure, but the views of at least some Africans could be put forward, as in 1916, when a show of loyalty over recruitment for the war effort secured for the inhabitants of the communes the final confirmation of citizenship. Nor was French West Africa without its proliferation of local societies, unions, and old-boys' associations, where matters of the moment could be discussed and grievances aired.

The crucial point came when the recognition of rights was no longer requested but demanded, and it was the Second World War of 1939–45 which brought matters to a head. The war itself acted as a catalyst, speeding up the economic and social changes which arose out of the very nature of the colonial systems. In the British possessions administrative pressure to produce more raw materials, closer government control of the economy, an increase in the growth rate of towns, and perhaps above all, inflation without a rise in incomes, served to arouse more people than ever before. Support for the nationalist leaders spread rapidly inland from the coast, and often this new support implied change to a more radical leadership. These developments marked the French colonies also, and were aggravated by the oppressive rule of administrations which for some years supported the collaborationist Vichy government and for the first time displayed gross racial discrimination against Africans. In both African empires literates perceived the defeats and humiliations suffered by Britain and France in the early years of the war, and at the end of the war both empires witnessed the return of thousands of ex-servicemen, men who were, in the words of the French politician Pléven, 'experiencing that aspiration towards a rebirth which characterizes the present age'. At the end of the war, then, conditions were ripe for change.

The post-war governments of Britain and France were aware of this. New constitutions were granted to the Gold Coast in 1946 and Nigeria in 1947, while a third, for Sierra Leone, was first suggested in 1947, though it was not in fact introduced until 1951. In acting like this the British government was taking the West African territories one step further along the path of colonial constitutional development which had been begun at the time of the Durham Report on Canada in 1839. The Gold Coast and Nigeria now enjoyed an unofficial majority of members in the Legislative Council, though only a few of these were directly elected on a limited franchise from the coastal towns, and the real centre of power was still the Governor and his Executive Council. Nevertheless, the West African territories were now following the same path as Canada, Australia, New Zealand, and South Africa had taken before them. With India, Pakistan, Ceylon, and Burma to act as further guides, a way had been opened through which the West African territories might ultimately pass.

At the end of the war France reconstructed her constitution, replacing the defeated and collapsed Third Republic with the Fourth. In doing so the position of the colonial territories had also to be reconsidered. The French Empire was replaced by the French Union, but though the former colonial 'subjects' now became citizens, their relationship with France was to be just as close as before. The principle of even ultimate independence was not entertained, and this had in fact been laid down firmly before the end of the war, at the conference held by the 'Free French', under the leadership of General de Gaulle, at Brazzaville in French Equatorial Africa during January and February 1944. This conference of administrators, while recommending extensive economic and social reforms in the African territories, still heartily endorsed the views of René Pléven, the Free French Commissioner for the Colonies, when he said:

We read at one time or another that this war must be ended with what is called a liberation of the colonial peoples. In the great colonial

France there are neither peoples to liberate nor racial discrimination to abolish. There are populations which feel themselves to be French, and which wish to take – and to whom France wishes to give – a greater and greater part in the life and democratic institutions of the French community. There are populations which we mean to lead, stage by stage, to personality, for the most mature to political freedoms, but who do not mean to understand any other independence than the independence of France.[3]

In 1945–6 representatives of the French West African territories took part in the two Constituent Assemblies at Paris, but they did so as members of the French Union who had a right to take part in debates on its structure, not as delegates seeking colonial independence. It was in response to the conservative reaction within France itself, culminating in the rejection of the first draft constitution for the Fourth Republic, a moderately liberal one in its attitudes to the colonies, that a nationalist movement emerged covering the whole of French West and Equatorial Africa.

The nationalist movements which arose in French and British West Africa at the end of the Second World War and just after, when potential leaders and potential followers came together, differed to the degree that the attitudes of France and Britain towards ultimate independence for their colonial possessions differed. The National Council of Nigeria and the Cameroons (N.C.N.C.) was founded in August 1944, and the United Gold Coast Convention (U.G.C.C.) in August 1947, in order to put pressure on the British government to speed up a process which it had already begun and the objective of which it in principle recognized – the pattern of development from a British colony or protectorate to an independent member of the Commonwealth. The Rassemblement Démocratique Africain (R.D.A.) was founded at the Bamako Conference of October 1946 as an organization which would represent the whole of French West and Equatorial Africa and seek to secure for Africans equality of treatment within the French Union.

The degree of pressure which each was able to bring varied considerably. In Nigeria the difficulties of organization encountered in such a large country, the failure of the N.C.N.C.

leaders to find a single issue around which to centre their campaign, the effective action taken by the administration against the more radical section of the movement, and above all, perhaps, the skill with which a new Governor, Sir John Macpherson, initiated constitutional and other reforms after 1948, combined to deprive the nationalist movement of the initiative by mid 1950. Elections were held towards the end of 1951 in accordance with the new constitution, and after a period of some confusion it became apparent that the three Regions into which Nigeria had been divided in 1946, and which had now been given governments of their own, were each to be controlled by a different party. The N.C.N.C. had won in the East, but two new parties, the Action Group and the Northern People's Congress (N.P.C.), had won in the West and North respectively. In the Gold Coast Dr J. B. Danquah and the moderate U.G.C.C. leaders found themselves gradually losing the initiative to the more radical leader whom they had brought back from the United Kingdom to act as party secretary, Kwame Nkrumah. In July 1949 Nkrumah broke with the U.G.C.C. and founded his own popular movement, the Convention People's Party (C.P.P.). The colonial administration had already been shaken by the rioting which followed firing upon ex-servicemen at the Christiansborg crossroads on 28 February 1948. As a result two commissions of inquiry were set up, one into the long-term causes of the riots and another, following the recommendations of the first, into revision of the constitution. The C.P.P. kept up its pressure and Nkrumah went to gaol, but in February 1951, after his party had won a majority of elective seats in the elections held to implement the new constitution, he was released to become Leader of Government Business.

In French West Africa the R.D.A. experienced much greater vicissitudes. For four years after its foundation, it worked closely with the French Communist Party in the hope of being able to bring more pressure to bear in Paris, but in the middle of 1947 the Communist Party left the French coalition government and went into opposition. From the end of 1948 the colonial administration was under orders to smash the allies of the Communists, and by October 1950 the R.D.A. could count its 'martyrs' in tens of dead and thousands of imprisoned. In that month Félix Houphouët-Boigny of the Ivory Coast, the R.D.A. leader, finally severed the movement's alliance with the Communist Party, but this was not soon enough to prevent French administrative pressure from being exerted to secure the defeat of all but a handful of R.D.A. candidates in the elections to the National Assembly of June 1951. The voice of West Africa was now heard there through the Indépendants d'Outre-Mer (I.O.M.), a parliamentary grouping whose most prominent leader was Léopold Senghor of Senegal, and another of whose leaders now became an Under-Secretary of State in the French government. Senghor had been a member of Lamine Guèye's Senegalese section of the French Socialist Party, and in 1946 he and his associates had refused to join Houphouët-Boigny in founding the R.D.A. The R.D.A. never gained a firm footing in Senegal, and, as so often before, that territory remained a law unto itself, witnessing a political change of great importance in 1948, when Senghor broke with Guèye and founded his own Bloc Démocratique Sénégalais, which in the 1951 elections proved strong enough to defeat the Socialists.

In retrospect the year 1951 can be seen to be a turning point. In British West Africa it witnessed a considerable step forward on the road to independence, with African ministers in Nigeria and the Gold Coast receiving a measure of real power and the nationalists having to adjust themselves to governmental responsibility. In French West Africa there had been no step forward, for there was as yet no recognized road to take. The R.D.A. had reached the nadir of its fortunes, but it had at last taken the decisive step of breaking with the Communists. From now on the attitude of the French government – whichever metropolitan parties might compose it – was to be much more favourable to colonial reform.

A Period of Adjustment

The period 1951–4 was one of rapidly changing attitudes, with both African political leaders and colonial administrators taking a fresh look at their positions. The Africans perhaps most drastically affected were the leaders in the Gold Coast and

Nigeria. Almost overnight – in the case of Kwame Nkrumah literally so – they had crossed the gulf between nationalist opposition and governmental responsibility. As yet that responsibility was severely limited, with the Governor still able to control events if he chose and with most of the senior civil servants in the new ministries still Europeans. Nevertheless, African party leaders were involved in the formulation and execution of policy, and were now held responsible by their own people for what the government did. All this placed a considerable strain both upon individual leaders and the parties themselves. Party discipline was shaken by conflict between those who sought to work within the new context and those who still thought in terms of opposing the colonial administration. In Nigeria prolonged crises shook the N.C.N.C. in 1952–3, while in the Gold Coast the radical Kwame Nkrumah found it necessary to purge his party of those who were now more radical than he. A remarkably amicable relationship in fact developed between him and the Governor, Sir Charles Arden-Clarke. In Nigeria, where ministers had been given less control over their departments, relations were not as good, and both the N.C.N.C. and the new Action Group (which was under pressure to prove itself as 'nationalist' a party as its rival) clashed intermittently with the British officials.

Despite occasional tensions in the Gold Coast, progress there in the period up to mid 1954 was remarkably smooth. In March 1952 Nkrumah became Prime Minister at the head of a Cabinet, instead of Leader of Government Business with a group of ministers. In June 1953 a further White Paper on constitutional reform appeared, and on 10 July the Prime Minister proposed his 'Motion of Destiny', calling for a further step towards independence. In April 1954 a new constitution granted internal self-government with the recognition of full ministerial responsibility, the Governor retaining only his emergency reserve powers and control over foreign affairs and defence. In June of the same year the C.P.P. won seventy-one seats out of 104 in a general election held on the basis of adult suffrage, but in the same election there appeared the first signs of a real opposition to the C.P.P., with the new Northern People's Party (N.P.P.), winning twelve seats. The significance of this was soon to become apparent.

Nigeria contrasted starkly with Ghana during this period. The difficulties that the parties experienced in re-adjusting themselves to the new situation were the prelude to a grave crisis and constitutional breakdown. In April 1953 an Action Group attempt to force the pace of progress towards independence by a motion in the central House of Representatives demanding independence in 1956 met with bitter opposition from the Northern members. The House adjourned in deadlock, the Northerners returned home, and the visit of an Action Group campaign team led to bloody riots at Kano in May. In July a constitutional conference opened in London, but it was adjourned in the following month when no agreement could be reached. Then, in January 1954, it was resumed in Lagos, this time was successfully concluded, and resulted in a new constitution, which came into force on 1 October. The basic obstacle had been the fear of the Northern representatives that their Region, relatively less developed than the others, especially in education, would be dominated by the East and West in an independent and unitary Nigeria. The answer found was the adoption of a federal constitution, which divided legislative powers between the Regions and the centre. Finance, the public service, the judiciary, and the public boards and corporations were all regionalized. The North was now free to develop at its own pace, and this settlement was reinforced by the agreement that all Regions should become internally self-governing at their own separate request, the East and the West each choosing the date 1956 for this, the North not yet naming a date. One further point of note is that the Southern Cameroons under British trusteeship now ceased to be administered as part of the Eastern Region and was given Regional status instead, with a government of its own, though with somewhat more restricted powers than the others.

Thus, by the end of 1954, Nigeria had moved constitutionally on to a federal path. From the point of view of the British administration this had much to recommend it; the solution was strongly supported by both the Action Group and the N.P.C., and even the N.C.N.C., the old advocate of Nigerian unity,

23

accepted it. Each party was now free to consolidate its hold over its particular Region, and in this it was greatly helped by the regionalization of finance and corporations. Although the Action Group was defeated in the West in the federal elections held towards the end of the year, it still retained control of the regional government, its most important asset.

In French West Africa the period 1951–4 was also one of adjustment. For the R.D.A. it was necessary to prove that the party had given up its bad old Marxist ways and become respectable. Its policy was now one of quiescence, following Houphouët-Boigny's maxim that 'in a period of crisis, inactivity is a positive attitude'. The party affiliated with the U.D.S.R., a small slightly left-of-centre group in the French National Assembly, and became loud in its protestations of loyalty to France.

'It is impossible to think that France and the Overseas Territorie[s] can pass from one another. Our destinies have been intermingled and a vital necessity commands us to survey completely the means and possibilities of the French Union . . . A page has turned; on the new one, completely blank, we write a resolution; to make Africa the greatest, finest, and most faithful territory of the French Union'.[4]

Gabriel d'Arboussier, the R.D.A. Secretary, was now expelled from the party, and he engaged in a lengthy public debate with Houphouët-Boigny, giving the latter a splendid opportunity to protest his new loyalty to France. The very small Senegalese section of the party, Djibo Bakary in Niger and Ruben Um Nyobe in Cameroun also refused to accept the break with the Communists, and in 1955 their severance from the R.D.A. became final. One group of radicals thus disappeared from the party, but a new radical force now emerged in the Guinea R.D.A. In late 1953 Sékou Touré, a young trade union leader, who had emerged as the leader of the party there, was elected to the Territorial Assembly. Although Touré supported the break with the Communists, he was a Marxist and an advocate of following a tough line towards the French. In June 1954 administrative influence was exerted to secure the election of his opponent in a by-election to the French National Assembly, and popular disturbances followed throughout the next year, all of them sternly repressed by the administration.

With the R.D.A. now quiescent and concerned primarily with protesting its loyalty to France, it was the I.O.M. which took the initiative in seeking changes in the structure of the French Union. At a congress held in April 1953 the West African members of the group, while protesting their loyalty, urged the adoption of a federal constitution for the Union, with greater powers for the Territorial Assemblies. The French governments of the period (some twenty of them in all succeeded each other in control of this crisis-torn Fourth Republic) had already shown themselves ready to grant reforms. In June 1950 overseas civil servants had been given terms of employment equal to those of their counterparts in France. In December 1952 a new Labour Code, first drawn up in 1944 and continually shelved since then, was promulgated. This provided for such reforms as equal pay for Africans and Europeans doing equal work, a minimum wage, and an eight-hour day. Assured now of the loyalty of the R.D.A. as well as of the I.O.M., the French governments were prepared to be more liberal. By April 1954 growing unrest in North Africa and above all the rapidly worsening position in Indo-China (Dien Bien Phu was to fall on 7 May) led to the contemplation of major constitutional reforms. In that month the Minister for Overseas France announced, amongst other things, that it was intended to grant the Territorial Assemblies more powers. The volatility of French domestic politics once again delayed the promulgation of these reforms for more than two years, but at least the principle had been recognized by 1954. As in British West Africa, the period of adjustment was over.

Diverging Paths

With the promise of reform in French Africa, the Gold Coast only one stage away from independence, and federalism fully established in Nigeria, distinct patterns were beginning to emerge in West Africa. The dialogue on independence between African nationalists and British administrators had begun in earnest, and it can now be seen that the same dialogue was about to begin in the French territories. Yet the debate was to take an increasingly different form in each area, with the paths to independence diverging.

From the middle of 1954 onwards, the dominance of the C.P.P. in the Gold Coast began to be challenged. Already before the June election the N.P.P. had come into existence, and so had the Moslem Association Party (M.A.P.) and the Togoland Congress Party. In September another regional party, the National Liberation Movement, arose in Ashanti to match the opposition in the Northern Territories. The C.P.P. was thus faced with a motley collection of opposing elements. Some were 'tribal' in nature, representing ethnic groups with a special interest – Dagomba or Mamprussi in the North, who did not like the modernizing ways of the C.P.P.; Ewe in Togoland, desiring unity with their brothers in French Togo; Ashanti who felt that the C.P.P. was the party of their former Fanti subjects. The M.A.P. was the party of the poverty-stricken Muslims in the *Zongos*, the strangers' quarters of the towns, many of them not from the Gold Coast at all but migrant workers from the French territories. To these were added spokesmen for more general interests, chiefs throughout the country (though most influential in Ashanti and the North) who disliked the radicalism of the C.P.P., intellectuals like Danquah who feared its appeal to the masses and its levelling policy. All these elements came together in the period 1954–7, to demand that when the Gold Coast became independent it was to have a federal constitution like that of Nigeria, with local interests enjoying some protection. Kwame Nkrumah listened, and in April 1956 his government accepted the report of Sir Frederick Bourne, which recommended regional assemblies with consultative powers and protection for the position of the Chiefs. In face of an opposition demand that the issue of a federal or unitary constitution be settled before independence, the British Colonial Secretary announced that another election would be held. Successful again, in July 1956, the C.P.P. won seventy-one of the 104 seats, but none the less, with some of the opposition leaders threatening secession, the Colonial Secretary in January 1957 forced further concessions from a C.P.P. government anxious above all else for rapid independence. Regional assemblies were now to have specified powers, and there were to be regional Houses of Chiefs as well. The C.P.P. government promised to attend to this within the twelve months following independence, and provisions were also written into the new independence constitution, to make any amendments on certain matters very difficult. It was with this constitution that the old Gold Coast became independent as the new Ghana on 6 March 1957, the first West African colonial territory to attain this status.

Nigeria, with its federal constitution and three major parties, each firmly entrenched in a particular Region, was in a quite different position. There the speed with which independence could be attained depended not on a dominant party's ability to beat off the challengers and at the same time satisfy the Colonial Office, but rather on the ability of three dominant parties to agree on a date. In the same month as Ghana became independent, this agreement was reached. At last the North, having already announced that it would seek internal self-government for itself in 1959, was prepared to fall in with the wishes of the other Regions and agree on 1959 as the year of Nigerian independence as well. In August 1957 the Eastern and Western Regions became self-governing, after a delay of a year caused by an investigation into Dr Azikiwe's African Continental Bank. In the meantime all three major parties had demonstrated their strength in Regional elections.

In May and June of 1957 another constitutional conference was held in London, and from the very first Nigeria's size and diversity posed problems. The Colonial Secretary proved even firmer than he had been with Ghana, refusing to give a 'blank cheque' for independence. It was agreed that Alhaji Abubakar Tafawa Balewa might now take the title of Federal Prime Minister, and that his Ministers should now constitute a Cabinet, but little else was achieved. Commissions were set up to study the problems of finance in a federal structure, the delimitation of constituencies for a new Federal election, and, perhaps of most immediate importance, the position of the various minority ethnic groups. Ever since power had begun to devolve in 1951 upon a major party within each Region, the main support for which came from the majority ethnic group of that Region, the Regional minorities had grown increasingly apprehensive about their future in an independent Nigeria. By 1957 the Action Group had taken up their cause, demanding the creation of at least three more Regions, or 'States', in the minority areas. This it wanted before independence, but when the constitutional conference resumed again in September 1958 to consider the reports of the commissions of inquiry, the party met with a rebuff. The Minorities Commission did not recommend the creation of any new states, and the Colonial Secretary accepted this view. The Action Group leaders had either to oppose the attainment of independence without new states, or concede the point, and they could not afford to be labelled as opposed to independence. The N.C.N.C. and N.P.C. were agreed that there were to be no new states carved out of their respective Regions, and the capitulation of the Action Group meant that now all were agreed on 1 October 1960, the date which the Colonial Secretary was prepared to accept for Nigerian independence.

The new Prime Minister had formed a 'National Government' in September 1957, by bringing the Action Group into coalition with his own party, the N.P.C., and the N.C.N.C. Nevertheless, the question of who was to be the recipient when full power was finally handed over by the British had yet to be decided. From October 1958 until December 1959 the attention of Nigerians was increasingly focused upon the federal election which was to settle this point. The Action Group made great efforts to exploit its links with the minorities and to persuade the peasants of the Northern emirates, the vast majority of whom were voting in a direct election for the first time, to use their votes against the N.P.C. as the party of the traditional rulers. The Action Group met with little success in its campaign, however, and won less seats than either of the other two parties, which had already agreed to form a coalition government if possible after the election. It was this government, composed of the N.P.C. and N.C.N.C., which accordingly led Nigeria into independence on 1 October 1960, with Dr Azikiwe, formerly the N.C.N.C. leader, becoming head of state as Governor-General on 16 November.

Ghana and Nigeria had thus followed their different paths to independence. Until 1951 they had progressed at an equal rate along the same path, reaching the stage of an unofficial majority in the Legislative Council together; but when actual governmental power had begun in some measure to be devolved upon African leaders, the Gold Coast had taken a different, more rapid path. After 1951 the divergence between them had become increasingly apparent, so that from 1957 onwards the new Ghana was tackling the first problems of independence, while Nigeria was still settling a date for independence itself. There are a number of explanations for this difference of pace. Sheer size and diversity were a great handicap to Nigeria, with the great size and relative isolation of the Northern Region only part, though a major part, of the problem. Moreover, largely because of these differences, the dialogue between nationalist leaders and the Colonial Office took different forms in the different countries after 1951. The C.P.P. managed, despite the challenge to it from 1954 onwards, to retain control of the government and the flow of events, successfully resisting the demand for a federal constitution. Nigeria, however, had three competing major parties, entrenched in Regions which had come into existence before two of the parties themselves, and the conflict between them led to a development of the federal principle, accepted by all three. The other participant in the dialogue, the Colonial Office, at times insisted on dictating the pace of constitutional development in both countries, but was on the whole more conservative in its attitude to Nigeria, regarding the Gold Coast as more developed and insisting on the complexity of Nigeria's particular problems.

Six months after Nigerian independence it was the turn of Sierra Leone. Held back at first by the quarrel between Colony and Protectorate, it was not until 1957 that a general election was held in which people from the latter area voted directly. Nevertheless, it was a Protectorate party, the S.L.P.P., which had first won a majority in 1951, and it was this party which retained control of events and conducted the dialogue with the Colonial Office which resulted in the adoption of a ministerial system in 1953 and the recognition of a Chief Minister in 1954. The S.L.P.P. was again returned to power in 1957, Dr Margai became Prime Minister in August 1958, and having survived internal disputes the S.L.P.P. formed a 'United National Front' with the opposition parties, in preparation for constitutional talks during April 1960. These resulted in independence on 26 April 1961. In May 1961, the Gambia, the last British possession in West Africa, where relations between Colony and Protectorate – along with its tiny size – had also determined the speed of development, was promised elections and internal self-government in not more than a year.

French West Africa: Loi Cadre, *Referendum, and Independence*

We last looked at the French territories during 1954, when the prospect of some constitutional reform was held out to them. The *Loi Cadre* ('Outline Law') was not in fact passed until June 1956, but the French governments in the meantime had demonstrated their willingness to undertake change by introducing a new Municipal Law in November 1955, and a system of family allowances for wage and salary earners from 1 January 1956. The *Loi Cadre* itself laid down the basic principles according to which far-reaching constitutional, administrative, and economic reforms were to be made, and in February 1957 a series of decrees implemented these. Powers of legislation were now divided into two groups – 'State' powers, reserved to the metropolitan country, and territorial powers. Included in the former were defence, foreign affairs, currency, and the economic development financed by FIDES (Fonds d'Investissement pour le Développement Économique et Social, founded in 1947). Among the latter were agriculture, health, primary and secondary education (except for curricula and examinations), internal trade, and the territorial civil service. In future the Territorial Assemblies were to be elected on a basis of adult suffrage. In each territory there was to be a Council of Government made up of ministers elected by the Assembly, and the man at the top of the elected list was to become Vice-President of the Council. Each minister would be individually responsible for a subject, and the whole Council might resign if it lost the Assembly's confidence. Thus, although the Governors were to be Presidents of the Councils and so retained substantial and effective reserved powers, for the first time a considerable measure of authority had begun to pass into the hands of the French-speaking African leaders, at a time when the Gold Coast was already on the eve of independence and Nigerian leaders had for the first time agreed on an independence date of their own.

At the same time the status of the trusteeship territories of Togo and Cameroun was changing. In August 1956 the first decree implementing the *Loi Cadre* made Togo an autonomous republic within the French Union, possessing a Prime Minister and legislative powers divided with France on the same pattern as that for the colonial territories, and in October a plebiscite, boycotted by the opposition parties, endorsed Togo's new status. A plebiscite held in British Togoland during May, however, had had results which were to be of greater ultimate significance. There a majority of the voters had opted for union with Ghana on the attainment of its independence, despite the strong opposition of the Ewe people. Since the Second World War a powerful movement seeking a union of the Ewe people, divided between French and British administration, had developed, and in 1956 it was the representatives of this movement who were outvoted in one part of Togo and who boycotted the plebiscite in the other.

The internal history of Cameroun is the stormiest of any country which will be dealt with in this book. As has already been noted the R.D.A. section there, Ruben Um Nyobe's U.P.C. (Union des Populations du Cameroun), opposed Houphouët-Boigny's rupture of the alliance with the Communists, favouring instead a militant attitude to the French administration. In June 1955 the R.D.A. Coordinating Committee, meeting in Conakry, formally expelled the U.P.C. section from the party, and in July the party was banned by the French administration. A year later, believing it impossible to attain independence and unify the two parts of the old Kamerun by peaceful means, Um Nyobe launched his party on a policy of armed insurrection. The French answer was two-fold, military action against the rebels (mainly in the Sanaga-Maritime and Bamiléké regions) and a new constitution for Cameroun, which came into force in May 1957 and provided for a Prime Minister and greatly increased legislative powers for the Assembly.

The period June 1956 to June 1957 thus saw constitutional changes of great significance in the countries under French administration. A measure of power was now passing to African leaders, some six years after this transfer had begun in the Gold Coast and Nigeria. The French Union still existed, and only students and other radicals spoke seriously of independence, but, as the French observer, André Blanchet, put it, there had been 'an effective displacement of the centre of gravity of French policy in an overseas direction'.[5] All this was bound to affect the political parties, faced for the first time with a prospect of power. The R.D.A. had now fully re-established itself. Already in the general election to the French National Assembly in January 1956 it had won a majority of the West African seats, and in February Houphouët-Boigny had become a minister in the French Cabinet. Now, in the elections to the newly-enlarged Territorial Assemblies held in March 1957, the R.D.A. won outright control of three of these (in the Ivory Coast, Soudan, and Guinea) and became the senior partner in a coalition Council of Government in a fourth, the territory of Upper Volta. Mauritania and Dahomey were controlled by local parties, and the two others, Senegal and Niger, by new inter-territorial parties, the Convention Africaine and the M.S.A. (Mouvement Socialiste Africain) respectively. The former, which replaced the I.O.M., was substantially Senghor's B.D.S., with the addition of small groups from outside Senegal, and the latter comprised the regrouped African sections of the French socialist party, the S.F.I.O. The inaugural conferences of both of these had been held in the same month, January 1957, and their formation is a clear indication of the shift in interest by the African leaders away from France towards their own continent, now that power was in fact to be won there. In January 1957 there was, indeed, a further indication of this trend, with the inauguration, at a third conference, of U.G.T.A.N. (Union Générale des Travailleurs d'Afrique Noire). Sékou Touré, acting on a suggestion he had first made in 1955, had led the African unions out of the Communist-dominated French Confédération Générale de Travail and established an autonomous African organization. Parallel developments were to be found in the Socialist and

Catholic trade unions, repeating on the level of organized labour what was happening in the political parties.

The process of change thus begun, with its potentialities for realignment, continued into 1958. The reforms introduced by the *Loi Cadre* had raised the whole issue of the relationship that should exist between France and its West African territories. In September 1957 the R.D.A. held a conference at Bamako, its first since 1949, and at a time when the C.P.P. government in Ghana was taking its first measures against the opposition (see Chapter 3) and a National Government was being formed in Nigeria, the major party in French West Africa was discussing whether the territories were to be developed separately or as a unit, and what was to be their future relationship with France. Before the conference met there were already significant differences of opinion among R.D.A. leaders. The *Loi Cadre* reforms had left a High Commissioner and Grand Council in Dakar with a federal public service responsible for implementing policy on 'State' matters, but the new emphasis on the individual territories had weakened the central powers. Felix Houphouët-Boigny – still a French cabinet minister – welcomed this. In a report to the Bamako conference he spoke of the need for 'the suppression as rapidly as possible of the intermediary organs between the central federal power and the territories, and, on the other hand, the regular affirmation each day of the personality and autonomy of the territories'. Sékou Touré – now Vice-President of the Council of Government in Guinea – did not welcome it. He wanted a close relationship between the territories and a federal executive in Dakar, a Government Council for the whole of French West Africa to match the one in each territory. Tension at the conference grew. It was prolonged for two extra days, sessions which Houphouët-Boigny did not attend. On the last day Sékou Touré, in his capacity as chairman, declared that 'Felix Houphouët-Boigny remains our President, but will carry to the government not his own ideas but those of the R.D.A.' The final resolution on federalism was reputedly redrafted seven times but emerged in a non-commital form.

Although the split had not become an open one, the battle within the R.D.A. was now joined. On the one side were those

THE NEW STATES OF WEST AFRICA

like Houphouët-Boigny who felt that the implication of the *Loi Cadre* reforms was the separate development of each territory, and the entering of each into its own individual relationship with France. It is not surprising that it was the Ivory Coast section of the party which was the strongest advocate of this view. The richest territory, accounting for nearly forty per cent of the annual exports of French West Africa and nearly ninety per cent of its dollar earnings in 1956, it found on the other hand that federal taxes levied from Dakar meant internal price increases of thirty to fifty per cent. The new Council of Government could see only benefit for an Ivory Coast allowed to go its own way and negotiate separately with France.

On the other hand Sékou Touré, leader of the third richest of the territories, found himself in agreement with Léopold Senghor, leader of the second richest, in asserting the importance of a primary federation of all territories, which would enter into a collective relationship with France. Senghor had for some years been the most critical of all the major African leaders towards the policies of the French governments, denouncing the *Loi Cadre* as offering only 'toys and lollipops'. Now he found his position close to that of the most radical of the R.D.A. leaders. In the latter part of 1957 and the early months of 1958 the regrouping of parties to form a united front for negotiations with France was in the air. By March 1958, however, the attempt had been wrecked upon the different attitudes to federation and the R.D.A.'s insistence on becoming the dominant partner in any merger. The Convention Africaine, M.S.A., and other local parties now fused to form the P.R.A. (Parti du Régroupement Africain), with the old rival Senegalese leaders, Senghor and Lamine Guèye, brought together again, and the party strongest in their territory. The stage was set for a contest in West Africa between the new P.R.A. and the old R.D.A., when in May 1958 the affairs of the French Union took a new and dramatic turn which overshadowed everything else.

On 13 May the French Army, dissatisfied with the continual political crises of the Fourth Republic, seized control of Algiers. Faced with the prospect of an invasion of France itself the government (of which Houphouët-Boigny was a member) collapsed, and General de Gaulle was called from retirement to form a new government. In July the draft constitution of his new Fifth Republic was published, and it was announced that a referendum on it would be held in September. For the Overseas Territories a number of solutions were proposed, but for those of West and Equatorial Africa there were in effect only two possible choices, autonomy within the new Community which de Gaulle offered as a replacement for the French Union, or else complete and immediate independence.

The referendum of 28 September 1958 was French Africa's crisis of decision. At last, with Ghana already independent for eighteen months and the Resumed Constitutional Conference engaged in fixing a date for Nigerian independence, the prospect of similar status was held out to the French-speaking territories. For Felix Houphouët-Boigny, now a minister in General de Gaulle's government, and his supporters the choice was easy; complete and immediate independence was unthinkable. Senghor's P.R.A. wavered. Supporting the idea of federation and then a negotiated relationship with France, it also feared the 'Balkanization' which might follow complete independence. In the end all the P.R.A.'s sections except that of Niger, led by Djibo Bakary, the former R.D.A. militant who was now Secretary of Senghor's new party, decided to vote 'Yes' for the new constitution. Bakary was unable, however, to carry the majority of the voters of Niger with him. At the final resolve only Guinea rejected General de Gaulle's proposals. The suspicion that the new Community was a disguise for the continuing dominance of France, and disappointment at the failure to create a West African federation inspired this fateful decision by Sékou Touré and the other leaders of his party, the P.D.G. Immediate independence followed the territory's overwhelming vote of 'No', and at the beginning of October Guinea joined Ghana as the second independent state in West Africa (apart, of course, from Liberia), the P.D.G. itself withdrawing from the R.D.A. In November a 'union' of Ghana and Guinea was announced, and the gulf between the English- and French-speaking territories had been crossed.

The referendum was a turning-point, just as the *Loi Cadre* had

35

been. The latter shifted the centre of gravity from Paris to Africa and turned the attention of many African leaders from federal union to individual territorial interests. The former introduced the word 'independence' into their vocabulary for the first time. The P.R.A. now began to negotiate for the formation of a West African federation, but the new word was always in its mind. In December 1958 Senegal, Soudan, Dahomey, and Upper Volta agreed to come together as the Mali Federation, named after the ancient empire of the Western Sudan, but by March 1959, internal instability and pressure from their wealthy neighbour, the Ivory Coast, had caused Dahomey and Upper Volta to change their minds. Senegal and Soudan then went ahead on their own, in March the new P.F.A. (Parti Fédéraliste Africain) was set up, and in April the Mali Assembly held its first meeting. In May a rival grouping appeared, when the Ivory Coast, Dahomey, Upper Volta, and Niger established their Entente Council, a looser association than the Mali Federation, mainly concerned with economic matters. Léopold Senghor and Modibo Keita, the Soudanese leader, were not prepared to leave matters there. They wanted independence for their new federation, within the Community if necessary, but certainly independence. As Senghor put it: 'Our goal is to establish a federal republic associated with France in a confederal community.' In September 1959 the P.F.A. executive, meeting in Dakar, decided to ask for independence and the transfer of Community functions to the Mali Federation. Article 86 in the Constitution of the French Republic, adopted in 1958, stated categorically that any member of the Community which subsequently became independent would then cease to be a member of the Community. In December the Community Executive at its sixth session decided, however, to allow the Mali Federation to become independent but remain a member, and following this decision the Malagasy Republic, far away off the east coast of Africa, decided to follow Mali's example. Early in April 1960 the necessary agreements were signed, and on 20 June the independence of the Mali Federation was proclaimed. On 20 August the Federation broke up, but Senegal and Soudan, with Soudan having taken for itself the new name of Mali, were now both independent.

The new status was contagious. Early in June 1960 the Senate of the Community had adopted a constitutional amendment allowing continued membership of the Community after independence. On the next day the four countries of the Entente group requested the granting of independent status to them, and at the end of July and the beginning of August the four followed the example of Senegal and Soudan. On 28 November Mauritania fell into line with the rest and became an independent republic. The Community as General de Gaulle had originally envisaged it was a dead letter. In just over two years it had been replaced by a series of separate agreements between France and individual independent republics, and by July 1961 the institutions, of the Community had been quietly abolished. In October 1961 the four Entente countries, as well as Senegal, Mali, Mauritania, Togo, and Cameroun all assumed control of their own military forces. The example of Guinea had proved too strong, and it is this which makes the decision of Sékou Touré and the P.D.G. to vote 'No' in September 1958 so important. Formal relationships with France – as opposed to the informal economic ties – were reduced to specific agreements on such matters as currency, the purchase of cash crops, the financing of economic development, technical assistance, and military matters. Moreover, these could be altered at any time the West African republics felt able to do so. Their economic dependence upon France made this less easy than it may sound, but relations with France were now the external relations of fully independent states, not agreements between partners in a community. In this respect their position had now come to resemble that of the former British possessions as members of the Commonwealth.

To complete this account the progress towards independence of two last states needs to be noted – Cameroun and Togo. We have already seen how each of them gained a measure of internal autonomy in 1956-7. In Togo the opposition led by Sylvanus Olympio, which had boycotted the plebiscite of October 1956, achieved power in the elections of April 1958. In Cameroun Ahmadou Ahidjo and his followers emerged as the dominant group after a crisis in February of the same year. In November the General Assembly of the United Nations

Organization voted to end the trusteeship of both territories in 1960. Progress for Togo was relatively smooth after this, with Olympio's government leading the country into independence, though without the long-dreamed-of Ewe reunion, in April 1960. Cameroun's path was more difficult, because of the continuing internal war against the U.P.C. Ahidjo's policy of conciliation and amnesty brought one section of the party, the 'legal' U.P.C., in from the bush, however, and in September 1958 Um Nyobe was killed. The most difficult problem remaining was the cause for which the U.P.C. leader had died, the unification of the two parts of Kamerun. The Security Council wanted a settlement of this problem before independence, and in the British Southern Cameroons the defeat of E. M. L. Endeley by John Foncha's K.N.D.P. in January 1959 brought a party into power which was far better disposed towards unification. Although part of the Federation of Nigeria, the Southern Cameroons took no part in the federal election in December of that year. On 1 January 1960 Cameroun became an independent republic, and in July Ahidjo and Foncha met for discussions which led to an agreement in principle to unite on a federal basis. In February 1961 plebiscites were held in both the Southern and Northern Cameroons. In the former a convincing majority chose unification with Cameroun. In the latter, administered as part of Northern Nigeria for over forty years, a plebiscite had already been held in November 1959, in which the majority of voters had chosen to defer the decision on their future status to a later date. That date had now been reached, and a majority of voters in the new plebiscite chose to remain with Northern Nigeria. President Ahidjo's government alleged the use of undue influence to achieve this result, and Ahidjo declared 1 June, the day on which the Northern Cameroons became the Sardauna Province of Northern Nigeria, a day of national mourning in Cameroun. The reunion of Cameroun and the Southern Cameroons was finally achieved on 1 October 1961, and the new federal state of Cameroun, combining for the first time areas which had been under separate French and British rule, came into being.

By the end of 1961, therefore, only the Gambia, Portuguese Guinea, and the islands of Fernando Po and Saõ Thome remained under colonial rule in West Africa. The first had by that date already been promised internal self-government after elections to be held not later than May 1962, and in Portuguese Guinea a nationalist movement had come into being. Liberia had of course enjoyed political independence since its foundation in 1847. The major part of the area, that which had been ruled by France and Britain, had moved rapidly and on the whole peacefully to independence in the years since the Second World War. The new *élites* which had come into being as a result of the European occupation had led the nationalist movements, and had entered into a dialogue with the colonial Powers which had ultimately resulted in independence for thirteen new states. These, together with Liberia, now make up a new state system, have varying relations with one another, as well as with the outside world, and possess many internal problems and characteristics in common. It is a study of these relations, problems, and characteristics which will occupy the remainder of this book.

2 The Heirs to the Throne

Along the road to independence, political power in the West African territories was transferred from one group to another, from the representatives of the colonial Powers to those who claimed to be the representatives of the People. The latter group was the *élite* which had emerged during the colonial period, new modern *élites* which now became 'heirs' to the colonial throne. It is these *élites*, these men (and, in a few cases, women) who now control the governments of the new states, and to a great extent, therefore, an understanding of these states must depend upon an understanding of their political *élites*.

The concept of an *élite* is a familiar one to West Africans. It is generally recognized that at the top of the social pyramid there is a group of the wealthy and powerful. The wealthy have usually made their fortunes through their activities in trading, transport, or construction. The powerful are pre-eminently the politically powerful. The two may be synonymous. Members of the *élite* may be powerful because of their wealth, and they may use their power further to increase their wealth. They may, however, be men without large personal fortunes who nevertheless wield power and influence because of their position in a dominant political party. The major characteristic of all of them is the relative ease with which they move in the modern world. They are undaunted – or appear so – by the complexities of modern economics and modern government. In their everyday lives they are called upon to write letters, use telephones, and draft memoranda, they own refrigerators and cars. They give the appearance of *using* the resources of the twentieth century, not of being at their mercy. In relation to the millions of their fellow

West Africans who cannot write letters, and who would find themselves at a complete loss if asked to use a telephone, the members of the new *élite* stand as intermediaries, as interpreters of the new political and economic systems which have developed in the last seventy or eighty years. Brought into power by the support of the mass of the people, whom they mobilized into a nationalist movement, the new *élites* in each country found themselves faced with the problems of first assuming, then wielding this political power. They found themselves also obliged to define their relationship with another *élite*, the traditional political *élite* which had existed before the European occupation and had survived the colonial period, though not unscathed.

The Impact of Colonialism

The period of European occupation in Africa can be viewed in two different ways. From one point of view it was an interruption in the development of African history, a development governed by social forces originating within the continent itself. In this view the new states which have rapidly succeeded the old colonial possessions can be regarded as legitimate successors of the states and cultures whose process of development was interrupted. The second view sees the new states as the successors rather of the colonial Powers, with the nature of their institutions and political life, as well as the economies upon which these depend, directly determined by the colonial system which went before. It is not necessary to accept either of these views in its entirety. Both can give valuable insights into the nature of the new West African states.

There can be little doubt that the impact of the colonial powers upon African traditional society was enormous. The Europeans came to West Africa determined to make changes, but with little understanding of what they were determined to change. As Mungo Park, the explorer, put it in his *Travels in the Interior Districts of Africa*:

. . . even the poor Africans, whom we affect to consider as barbarians, look upon us, I fear, as little better than a race of formidable but ignorant heathens.

The impact of colonial rule was formidable because of the

far-reaching nature of the processes of economic and social change which it initiated. It is essential to understand these, since the political *élite* of the present day is largely their creation. Yet it is essential also to remember the power of tradition. The colonial rulers were also (with a few distinguished exceptions) ignorant, for they formulated their policies and promoted them with little knowledge of pre-colonial history and traditional society, though it was these which were largely to determine the reaction of Africans to the policies themselves. The Hausa peasant in Northern Nigeria accepted the rule of the British because they had 'repaired the world', put an end to fighting among the emirs, slave-raiding, and the counter-attacks of the 'pagan' peoples who were the chief source of slaves. The peasants of Guinea supported Sékou Touré from the first because he was descended from the Muslim leader Samōri, who had fought the French. The modern *élite* is equally swayed by what it conceives to be history and tradition. How else can the adoption of the name of one of the ancient empires of the Western Sudan – Mali – for the abortive federation of Senegal and Soudan, or that of another – Ghana – for an independent Gold Coast, be explained? Like the new states themselves, the members of the dominant *élite* are the products of extremely complex patterns of interaction between traditional societies, evolved over many centuries, and the forces set in motion by colonial rule.

What then were the processes of economic and social change which created the modern *élites*? First of all it must be remembered that in West Africa these changes were the work of three main groups of Europeans, the traders, the administrators, and the missionaries. Their interests were not uniform, and at times were even in conflict. The traders, first upon the scene, were naturally interested in the profits to be made in an area in which few of them would ever have lived by choice. The missionaries, also early arrivals, were anxious to save the souls of the heathen. The administrators, agents of the political power which in the end was forced to intervene to protect the interests of the others, were concerned above all else with law and order. This last, of course, was a prerequisite for the activities of the traders and missionaries as well, and so the necessity for it was one thing upon which all three main groups could agree. One other matter was commonly agreed upon, the importance of inducing the African to direct his energies towards new forms of productive labour, in return for which he might hope for some cash reward. The company agent wanted a regular supply of products for export – ground-nuts, cotton, cocoa, coffee, rubber, palm oil and palm kernels, timber, and the rest. The mining companies needed labour for the production of tin, gold, diamonds, and other minerals. The administrative officers knew that energies directed towards such work would not be employed in inter-village warfare, and would instead earn the money for taxes which the administration needed to pay for its own existence. The missionary held that virtue and steady labour had always gone hand in hand. For his own part the African, urged to a life of Christian virtue in those places where missions had been planted, and faced everywhere with the dire consequences of opposition, saw that in the modern world he must turn his innate capacity for hard work in new directions. Only in that way might he earn the money to buy the new cloth, bicycles, and corrugated iron sheets for roofing which the trading companies' stores offered for sale. There were sporadic attempts to resist direct taxation, such as the Sierra Leone 'Hut Tax War' of 1898 or the 'Women's Riots' in the eastern provinces of Nigeria during 1929, but in much of British and French West Africa the peasant farmers soon settled down to the industrious cultivation of cash crops, a monument to peasant enterprise of which the development of the Gold Coast cocoa industry from the 1880s onwards is merely one impressive example.[1]

In West Africa there was a tradition of trade with the European extending back to the fifteenth century contacts with the Portuguese. Places like Gorée, Cape Coast, and Calabar had been centres of trade in commodities such as slaves, ivory, and gold-dust for centuries. Whole kingdoms, Dahomey and Benin the most famous, had flourished upon trade with foreign merchants, and the coastal areas with their hinterland, the whole of the 'forest belt' in fact, were no strangers to Europeans and European merchandise. The extension of direct political control by the Powers over West Africa, however, inevitably had a profound effect upon the pattern of this trade. The old independent kingdoms were destroyed, and many of the African traders found themselves unable to compete with the European trading companies once they lost their political control over access to the interior sources of supply. Yet African traders were not eliminated from the colonial economy. None of them could compete with the United Africa Company or the Compagnie Française de l'Afrique Occidentale. Very few of them could even attain the fortunes of Lagos Yoruba merchants like J. B. Coker or Akinola Maja. Nevertheless, as produce-buyers, agents of the foreign firms, and retailers of imported goods, African merchants were active along the coast and inland. The extension of direct political control by the colonial Powers may often have destroyed the old indigenous trading group, and the upper levels of the economy were certainly controlled by the great trading companies, but there remained a place for Africans in the middle and lower levels.

Opportunities for African traders, indeed, increased rather than diminished, for the colonial administration encouraged the growth of cash crops, and these required middlemen between the peasant producers and the exporting companies. Despite competition from Lebanese and European traders (the latter found at this level more frequently in French than in British West Africa) the local middlemen were able to find an important place here. It is a factor of considerable significance that, unlike the situation in East Africa where almost everything was for years left to the Indians, in West Africa the demand of the colonial economy for small-scale traders was met by indigenous enterprise.

Cash crops must be transported to the coast, and colonial administrators must be able to move troops rapidly in the event of serious disturbances. Here railways were of the greatest importance. In Senegal the French linked Dakar with the Niger by 1924. By the outbreak of the First World War Conakry and Kankan had been linked, but the line from Abidjan into the interior reached Bobo-Dioulasso only in 1934 and Ouagadougou in 1954. The other main line, from Cotonou to Parakou in Dahomey, was not completed until the mid 1930s. The first railway built by the British in the Gold Coast ran from the gold mines at Tarkwa to the port of Sekondi, while by 1903 Kumasi, centre of the Ashanti rising in 1900, had been connected with Accra. In Nigeria the line from Lagos reached Ibadan in 1900, and the cotton and groundnut collecting centre of Kano in 1911. By the mid 1920s Kano was also linked to the other main funnel of Nigerian exports, Port Harcourt. In the thin strip of the Gambia the river provides an effective substitute for a railway, while Sierra Leone boasts of one line, from Freetown to Pendembu. A system of feeder-roads also developed, focusing on the towns along the railways and becoming of greater importance with the introduction of transport lorries in increasing numbers from the 1930s onwards.

All of this led to far greater mobility. Individual West Africans have always been great travellers; now travel was made easier and quicker, and greater distances could be covered. Protected by the law and order of the colonial system and using its Dakar–Niger railway, a Dioula trader from Senegal could now, if he wished, travel with relative ease between Dakar and Bamako, a distance of 750 miles. If jobs were to be had in a distant area, it was now possible for migrant labourers to travel there and work for the cash they needed. The seasonal movement of the *navétanes* from Upper Volta into the Ivory Coast and Gold Coast to work as labourers during the harvesting of the cocoa and coffee crops became a permanent feature of French West Africa's economy. In 1945 some 460,000 people journeyed on the Volta River ferries into and out of the Gold Coast, and by 1954 the figure had risen to 1,800,000.

The establishment of colonial administrative systems, the collection of cash crops, the sale of new imported goods, the development of communications, all implied the rapid growth of towns, and this was true whether the town was of pre-colonial foundation, like Porto Novo and Kano, or new, like Dakar or Port Harcourt. Protected by the new law and order, attracted by the prospect of new sources of work, travelling on the new roads and railways, people streamed from the villages to swell the urban population. Many of them later returned to their native villages, but others remained. Table I shows the estimated growth of certain West African towns during the colonial period.

45

Table I   Growth of Selected Towns

Town	Population (to the nearest thousand)		
Thiès (Senegal)	1921: 6,000	1931: 11,000	1952: 50,000
Kano	1921: 50,000	1931: 97,000	1953: 130,000
Dakar	1921: 32,000	1931: 54,000	1952: 257,000
Port Harcourt	1921: 7,000	1931: 15,000	1953: 72,000

Whether a man settled in a town permanently or not, his life there was an invaluable training in the ways of the new modern world, with its law-courts and form-filling, sanitary regulations and book-keeping. It would be absurd to suggest that all members of the modern *élite* are the products of life in the towns. To a remarkable extent, however, the leaders of modern West African society constitute a 'bourgeoisie', if we take that term in its original, medieval sense, as meaning those whose chief characteristic is their association with a 'bourg'. Apart from the schools, the towns were the major channels by which the new forces of change could be brought to bear on the individual, in an environment quite different from the traditional one to which he was accustomed.

The most decisive factor of all, however, was the availability of modern education. In the colonial days such an education was generally the gateway to a rewarding career. This is not to say that an illiterate person could not be rich and powerful; there were, in particular, many important traders who had had no modern education. Nevertheless, however important may have been their financial contributions to the nationalist parties, it was not the illiterate traders who became the modern political *élite*. Participation in modern government requires at any rate a nodding acquaintance with the mysteries of reading, writing, and arithmetic. Of course this does not mean that all those who received an education in the period up to 1950 or thereabouts are now members of the political *élite* in West Africa. What it does mean is that, with very few exceptions, the men who now fill positions of political and administrative authority are those who during the colonial period were able to gain access to the limited education available, and were then able to invest their new asset in a new career.

Two aspects of education in the colonial period must be remembered. First of all, its availability was very limited until the late 1940s, when Britain and France both launched their rather belated programmes of development in face of nationalist pressures. In the British territories education was for long left primarily to the missions. In the Gold Coast during 1930 only just over eleven per cent of the estimated total number of pupils were in government schools. By and large, therefore, the availability of education in British West Africa depended upon the distribution of missions and the date at which they had arrived in a given area. In some regions, the British administration actually discouraged the missions, lest they should offend Islamic susceptibilities, and so there were very few schools there; such was particularly the case in the traditional states of Northern Nigeria. In French West Africa the secularist traditions of the Third Republic caused it to reserve most educational activity to itself; the figures for the Gold Coast given above may be compared with those for 1934 in the neighbouring Ivory Coast, where private schools accounted for only some twenty-one per cent of total pupils. The overall effect of this difference in policy was that even less children were educated in the French territories than in the British. In 1934 some 60,000 children were at school in French West Africa out of a total population of about 14,000,000; the figures for British West Africa was 315,000 out of 25,000,000.[2] As in the British, so also in the French territories, schools were unevenly distributed and Senegal, as a result of its longer contact with France, had far more facilities than any other French possession in the area.

The second point to be remembered is that not only were there few schools, unevenly distributed, but that education in the main was also directed to a limited purpose. The missions wanted teachers, catechists, and lay preachers, while the administration and trading companies wanted clerks; few positions of greater eminence were open to Africans under the colonial system. There were a few secondary institutions of a high standard – the École William Ponty, Achimota College, Fourah Bay

College – but only a very few of the small minority who received any education at all were able to attend these. Some young men, of course, travelled abroad, to France and Britain, in search of higher education and a number later went to the U.S.A. Neither the French nor the British governments prevented this, provided that the students could raise the necessary funds. Indeed, both colonial powers were eager to create a group of influential men who would support their rule and act as intermediaries between the administration and the mass of the people. The French policy of assimilation sought most consistently to create this group of *évolués*, since under the system of Indirect Rule the British relied more upon the support of the chiefs, but neither colonial Power experienced much success with this policy. Each system produced its conservative Blaise Diagnes and Sir Kitoyi Ajasas, but it also produced doctors, lawyers, and other professional men who became nationalist leaders and subsequently important members of the contemporary political *élite*. Nevertheless, potentialities for conflict between these more highly educated men and those who were forced to remain content with the education they could get in West Africa have existed in the past, and still exist. At least one important West African country – Ghana – has witnessed a shift of political leadership away from a more highly educated to a less highly educated *élite*.

Circumstances may differ in each of the new states of West Africa, but the historical process in every one has been the same. In each a new *élite*, a product of the social and economic changes of the colonial period, has replaced the colonial power as the wielder of authority. The establishment of law and order, the fostering of cash crops and the circulation of money, the improvement of communications, the growth of towns, modern education, all these created new avenues of social mobility, in addition to – and to some extent replacing – those which existed traditionally. A group of people found it possible to improve their social position by accepting the new conditions and exploiting them. In the colonial situation, however, such upward mobility was limited, and as a result these 'new men' rallied the nationalist movement, sponsored it, and led it, with the results seen in the previous chapter. When the time came for power to be transferred, in the late 1950s and early 1960s, they were the heirs to the colonial throne; the scope of their mobility had thus been infinitely extended.

Islam, Tradition, and the Modern Élite

So far the development of the modern political *élite* has been discussed solely in terms of the European impact upon West Africa. To leave it at this would, however, be a grave distortion of historical truth. The position of the modern *élite* is not a result of this impact alone. The weight of tradition is still felt very heavily in West Africa, and we have already noted that it must be – and is – taken into account by the new rulers. The European penetration of a very large part of West Africa is of very recent date. As one scholar has put it:

The fact is that the real conflict between African and European institutions was hardly felt anywhere in West Africa more than 200 miles from the coast before the 1880's. This leaves an area of nearly 700,000 square miles southward of the latitude of Lake Chad un-accounted for during the greater part of the nineteenth century in so far as the 'European influence' type of theme is concerned. This vast tract of savannah land, while not entirely cut off from the outside world, continued indeed to live its own life quite untroubled by European influence until it was conquered in the last twenty years of the century.[3]

Moreover, the area in which European influences made themselves felt at a relatively late date is also the area in which another influence, also originally alien but established for a much longer time, that of Islam, is strongest. The Arab conquest of North Africa in the seventh century A.D. had laid West Africa open to Islamic influences via the Saharan trade routes, but the decisive act seems to have been the conquest of the empire of Ghana by the Muslims of the Murābitūn movement in 1076 and the consequent dispersal of the Soninke people.[4] The following nine centuries have seen Islam spread throughout West Africa, penetrating the coastal forest belt and reaching the sea in Guinea, Senegal, and among the Yoruba people of Western Nigeria and Dahomey. Its main influence has remained north of this belt, however, in the desert and savannah lands.

In much of West Africa, then, the influence of Islam is a factor entering into the development of the modern states and their dominant *élites*. Nor has this factor by any means been static. Indeed, the century before the European conquest began in earnest – the period, that is, from about 1785 to 1885 – was a period of reform and revival as important in their implications as the effects of the European penetration of the coastal belt. As the article quoted above points out:

> The history of the West African savannah in the nineteenth century has its own independent theme; and this consists in a series of revolutionary movements which radically changed the social and political complexion of the whole zone during the hundred years or so before the establishment of the European governments.[5]

When the French expeditions pushed up the Senegal River and down the Niger, and the agents of the Royal Niger Company penetrated Northern Nigeria, making treaties where they could, using force where they thought necessary, it was the states established as a result of these Islamic revivalist movements with which they had to deal. The first of these movements had been that led by 'Uthmān dan Fodio, the Fulani scholar and religious teacher, who between 1804 and 1810 had overthrown the Habe (Hausa) rulers of Northern Nigeria, accusing them of a reversion to heathen practices, and had then established his own empire, with its capital at Sokoto. The second had been led by a follower of 'Uthmān, Ahmadu Lobo, who had established a theocratic state in Massina, in modern Mali, about the year 1810. Ahmadu's successors had then in their turn been defeated and overthrown in 1862 by the third of these Islamic leaders, *al-hājj* 'Umar, who had declared a *jihād*, or holy war, in the Fouta Djallon (in modern Guinea) in 1848. Lastly must be mentioned the Soninke–Malinke conqueror Samōri, who between about 1870 and 1890 established and ruled a large empire in upper Guinea and northern Ivory Coast, resisting the advance of the French until he was captured and exiled by them in 1898. All of these men sought to restore the purity of Islamic practice and to spread it among the 'unbelievers'. In doing so they greatly strengthened the faith on the very eve of the European conquest, and to some extent their resistance or that of their successors tended to identify Islam with opposition to colonial rule.

In much of West Africa throughout the colonial period, therefore, there existed a rival cultural tradition strong enough to withstand that of Europe. This meant that in some areas, such as Northern Nigeria or the Fouta Djallon, an educational system existed which could act as a rival to that introduced by the British or French, and which did not serve as a channel for the introduction of new ideas. Politically, too, the strength of Islam meant the survival in some areas of traditional systems of government and traditional rulers. In English-speaking West Africa, where the British administration built the traditional political *élite* into its system of Indirect Rule, the descendants of dan Fodio in Northern Nigeria retained some measure of authority, while even the desire of the French to reduce the significance of the chiefs could not prevail against the Fulani of the Fouta Djallon or the Hausa rulers in Niger. Even in some non-Muslim areas the traditional rulers proved to have strong powers of survival – the *Moro Naba* of the Mossi, for instance, or the Ashantis' *Asantehene*. This survival of the traditional *élite* has posed a problem for its modern counterpart. As heirs to the throne, what attitude should the new men adopt towards the old? How far is the continuing authority of the traditional *élite* compatible with progress as the new rulers see it?

It must not be thought, however, that the influence of Islam has been only a conservative one. There is a democratic aspect of Islam, deriving its inspiration from the brotherhood of all believers and a particular interpretation of the rule of the Prophet and the early caliphs, which allows its followers to take their place among the most radical of the modern *élite*. Thus the leaders of Sékou Touré's P.D.G. in Guinea, whose experience was mainly in trade union organization and who had been much influenced by Marxism, were nevertheless able to claim that:

. . . we are in the pure line of Islam, conquering because humane and charitable, when we denounce with energy the abuses of certain powerful people, chiefs through imposition upon the people, administering by oppression, beating, robbing, fleecing the orphan, the widow, and even the dead, despite the mile-long rosary which they perpetually tell in order to put on a hypocritical air of false devotion.[6]

Similarly, the Northern Elements' Progressive Union (N.E.P.U.) in Northern Nigeria and Djibo Bakary's Sawaba ('Freedom') Party in Niger both sought to appeal to such democratic traditions against their more conservative opponents, who possessed the support of the traditional rulers, though without success in either case.

In areas where Islam has long been established, then, in northern Cameroun, Northern Nigeria, Niger, Mali, Guinea, Senegal, and Mauritania, it has profoundly affected the process of *élite*-formation produced by the social changes of colonial rule. In some of them it offered an alternative cultural tradition, and even indigenous political systems which survived foreign rule and provided ways of attaining power and influence other than the purely modern ones. These traditional systems adopted such modern appurtenances of government as telephones, filing systems, typewriters, and even the ballot box without giving up their pre-colonial view of the political process – the importance they attached to established authority and hierarchies. Such was broadly true of northern Cameroun, Northern Nigeria, Niger, and Mauritania. In Guinea, as noted above, and also in Mali, another Islamic tradition successfully fused with modern ideas, and it is interesting that here the single-party systems appear unusually strong. The remaining country, Senegal, provides an interesting case-study, as possessing a political system in which a modern *élite*, produced mainly by the process of social change, is still heavily dependent upon the support of Muslim religious leaders like Abdoul Aziz Sy of the Hāfiziyya Tijāniyya order.

Patterns of Power

As has now become apparent, there are considerable differences between the modern political *élites* of the different states in West Africa. The nature of the interplay between traditional and modern *élites* has varied, the former sometimes playing a very significant part in the development of the political system during the last years of colonial rule. The process is complicated by the fact that, in the 'coastal' territories, the effects of European contact went through two separate stages. First of all, beginning to emerge even before the establishment of formal political control by the Powers, a new *élite* developed in the coastal towns – in the Senegalese communes, in Bathurst, Free-town, Monrovia, Sekondi, Cape Coast, Accra, Lomé, Cotonou, Porto Novo, Lagos, Calabar. This may be termed the 'Creole' *élite*, borrowing a term from Freetown. There, and in a number of other towns, the basis of this group was formed by liberated slaves, returned to their native continent but by no means necessarily to their native land. Although they intermarried with local families, the peculiar nature of their experience meant that their adoption of a European mode of life, European education, and European attitudes was extensive and whole-hearted. (This penchant for things European, however, was also true of towns like Dakar in which the freed-slave element was not the pre-dominant one). Until the end of the Second World War, and indeed for some years after it, this Creole *élite* remained socially dominant, looking down upon the 'natives' of the 'hinterland' and holding most of the higher administrative positions open to Africans. Rarely did its representatives question the validity of colonial rule as such; bodies like the National Congress of British West Africa tended rather to demand the granting of extended rights to Africans, with equality of treatment.

The effects of European contact reached their second stage with the emergence of the modern nationalist movements. The process of social change had progressed far enough by the 1940s for leaders to appear who were not sentimentally attached to European ways of life and who were able to recruit followers from the 'hinterland'. As a result, the period of nationalist re-action against the British and French was also the period when the initiative swung inland from the coast. Senegal provides a clear example of this in the period 1948–51, when Senghor broke with Lamine Guèye and built up the overwhelming power of his B.D.S. by appealing to the 'subjects' of the interior against the 'citizens' of the coast. In Sierra Leone the victory of Milton Margai's S.L.P.P. in the first elections of 1951 clearly marks the shifting of the political balance from the Colony area to the much larger and less-developed Protectorate. The same sort of shift can be seen in southern Nigeria – with politics ceasing to be centred on Lagos – and in the Gold Coast. The latter is of special interest, since there the Creole *élite* had actually itself launched the modern nationalist movement in the form of the U.G.C.C., but lost control of it to Kwame Nkrumah and his more radical and 'populist' C.P.P. Liberia is exceptional. There, political power has never slipped from the hands of the Creoles, and in the absence of a colonial Power to spur on a nationalist movement, no rival group has emerged which has been able to challenge the old *élite*.

In many ways, then, the development of modern nationalism and the gradual transference of power to Africans has meant a kind of 'race to the hinterland'. Votes have meant power, and most votes were to be found there. Often, too, the first party to arrive and capture these votes has retained them, and thus has retained power. Despite several changes of name Senghor's present U.P.S. (Union Progressiste Sénégalaise) is the same party as his old B.D.S. The S.L.P.P. in Sierra Leone, the C.P.P. in Ghana, and the N.C.N.C. in Eastern Nigeria have each enjoyed more than a dozen years of power.

Nevertheless, despite the complicating historical shift of power from a 'Creole' to a 'modern' *élite* in some of them, the new states of West Africa may most conveniently be classified according to the relationship between the traditional and modern *élites* during the last decisive decade before independence, when it was being decided who would inherit political power from Britain or France. It was this relationship – it may reasonably be argued – that determined the nature of the political system which emerged at independence. If this criterion is adopted, a spectrum of states may be established, ranging from those in which the traditional *élite* remained relatively powerful to those in which it failed to play any significant political role.

The three states in which the traditional *élite* played the most important part are predominantly Muslim ones, the Islamic Republic of Mauritania, Niger, and Northern Nigeria.* In all three the dominant political leaders initially derived their power from their membership of, or close association with, traditional

* Strictly speaking, of course, Northern Nigeria is not a state in its own right, but a Region in a Federation. Nevertheless, from our point of view here, Nigeria is something of an historical accident, the result of the grouping together by a colonial Power of two very different areas with very different patterns of develop-

ruling groups or religious leaders. In each of them parties drawing their inspiration from other sources – reformist Islam or
Western European ideas – have failed to gain any widespread
support. Even in Niger, where Djibo Bakary, the Marxist trade
union leader, was in power for a time (March 1957 to December
1958), his cause was lost once the traditional rulers had swung
against him.

In our spectrum of states these three merge into another
group in which traditional authority has been of great importance,
not because of its continuing influence upon the actions of the
ruling group, but because at the decisive point in the struggle for
power between rival heirs to the throne it was the support of
this authority which decided the issue. Such was the case in
Cameroun, where Ahmadou Ahidjo, by swinging his Union
Camerounaise against André Mbida, his former ally, in January–
February 1958, was able to replace him as Prime Minister.
Ahidjo could command the firm support of his regionally based
party at a time when the rest of the modern political *élite* was
divided into quarrelling factions and faced with a serious rebellion, led by some of its radical members. He was able to retain
power in a difficult situation because of his strong support in the
North (his party won all forty-four seats there, unopposed, in
the election of April 1960) and use of governmental power (the
Assembly was suspended for a time in 1959, and in 1962 opposition leaders were imprisoned). Son of a Fulani chief and a
former leader of the *Jeunes Musulmans*, Ahidjo had been able to
count upon the support of an area where traditional authority was
still strong enough to ensure party solidarity and effective action.

The rise of Hubert Maga to power in Dahomey provides a
second example. Again a man of the North, part Bariba and
recognized as a modern leader by a people among whom traditional authority is still strong, he first became prominent as a
leader of the Group Ethnique du Nord. In Dahomey during
1958, as in Cameroun, rivalry between southern-based parties

---

ment. In practice the British administration tended to treat the two as separate
entities, despite the 'amalgamation' of 1914, and the constitutional development of
modern Nigeria has had as one of its main themes the reconciliation of the North and
South.

led to political crisis, so that Maga's party (now the Mouvement Démocratique Dahoméen) was brought into a coalition government to lend it stability. In April 1959, in an even tenser situation, he became a compromise head of government. A third crisis in November 1960, with serious strikes and a trip to the South by Northern supporters of Maga to form a guard around his home, enabled him to manoeuvre between the southern parties, dropping one set of allies and acquiring another. After this the use of State power against the opposition party, Press, and trade unions confirmed him in control. Once again, in a conflict between potential heirs to the throne, a strong basis of support in an area where traditional authority ensured cohesion could be a great advantage to a member of the new *élite*.

If the Federation of Nigeria is taken as a whole it may be added to this group of states. There, too, traditional authority has remained strongest in the North, and the party which controls the North, the Northern People's Congress, has been able to extend this control over the entire Federation. The decisive moment was the federal election of December 1959, which decided the balance of political power on the eve of independence. The N.P.C., having used its links with traditional authority to win most of the seats in the North, was able to become the dominant partner in the coalition federal government, to reserve the office of Prime Minister for one of its leaders, and to consolidate its position during the next few years. Yet, although this coming to power of the N.P.C. at the federal level provides yet another example of the great asset which traditional authority has been under certain circumstances, it must also be remembered that in Nigeria the N.P.C. was benefited by an historical accident. The decisive moment, as has been said, was a federal election, and the Northern Region had been allocated more than half the seats in the federal House of Representatives, because it was believed to possess more than half the population of the Federation. The census carried out in May 1962, however, cast grave doubts on this belief, though the N.P.C.'s dominance of the central government enabled it to have the census itself declared null and void. Whether the N.P.C. can retain its dominance under these circumstances without serious challenge remains to be seen, and in this sense Nigeria is one of the least stable of the West African states, since the final struggle for power has yet to be fought.

In the middle of our spectrum is the third group, the largest, made up of states where the modern political *élite* has found it advantageous to come to terms with traditional authority, though at no point has the latter been the decisive factor in the struggle for power. In some of these states traditional authority has been of great importance, as in the Upper Volta election of April 1959, when the *Moro Naba*, paramount chief of the Mossi, swung his influence behind Maurice Yaméogo. In Sierra Leone the dominant S.L.P.P. has consistently used the chiefs as its local agents, and in return has guaranteed their place in the modern governmental structure; a quarter of the seats in the House of Representatives is reserved for chiefs. Elsewhere, as in Western Nigeria or the Ivory Coast, the support of the traditional rulers has been useful to the modern *élite*, but it has been made amply clear that the *élite* remains the master.

Throughout West Africa, in fact, there is a tendency for the modern *élite* to use traditional authority in order to help establish support for the new régimes during the crucial early years, but at the same time gradually to weaken it. As will be shown in further detail later on, the new rulers are not prepared to tolerate any group able to claim a rival allegiance, and this applies to traditional chiefs and religious leaders as well as to trade unions and student organizations. This is true even in the states where the modern *élite* is linked most closely with the traditional, as in Northern Nigeria where in May 1963 the Northern People's Congress regional government found it necessary to force the abdication of the Emir of Kano, one of the three most powerful traditional rulers, and replace him with someone more amenable. If the chiefs are ever to put up a fight, it is likely to be in one of these states, though interestingly enough it is Senegal which provides us with the only example of this to date. There the attempt to resist came relatively early, in the period before independence, when some of the religious leaders tried unsuccessfully to launch the Parti de la Solidarité Sénégalaise in February–March 1959.

At the other end of the spectrum from Northern Nigeria, Niger, and Mauritania are three states, Guinea, Mali, and Ghana, in which the dominant political party set out from a quite early date to weaken the power of the traditional *élite*. Thus in Guinea one of the first major acts of Sékou Touré's P.D.G. after gaining a measure of power in 1957, was to depose several chiefs, abolishing those at the canton level altogether at the end of the year. This action was especially directed against the Fulani chiefs of the Fouta Djallon, who had been the main opponents of the nationalists and supporters of the French.

In Mali the Union Soudanaise–R.D.A. has taken a stand similar to that of the P.D.G. Only the chiefs of the nomadic peoples in the northern desert areas have been left alone, to act as agents of local administration in the same way that they did under the French. Yet the party's monopoly over all political activity now makes it impossible for these, and any other chiefs or religious leaders, to influence the turn of events. As Madeira Keita, Mali's Minister of the Interior, has put it:

> The rallying of these chiefs is positive on the political level because this rallying neutralizes them and does not automatically give them a role to play in the party.[7]

In Ghana the C.P.P. found it more difficult to subordinate traditional authority to its own, for whereas the French colonial administration had tried wherever possible to appoint 'chiefs' who in fact possessed no traditional authority, the British had confirmed the traditional chiefs and used them as their agents. The radical message of the C.P.P. after 1949 was accordingly no more acceptable to the chiefs than to the old Creole *élite*, and in the period from 1954 to 1957, when Kwame Nkrumah's party was meeting its strongest opposition, chiefs were often heavily involved. The National Liberation Movement in particular received whole-hearted support from the *Asantehene* and the other Ashanti chiefs, as did the Northern People's Party from the chiefs in the Northern Territories. When these parties were crushed, therefore, with the rest of the opposition, in the years immediately after independence, retribution was visited upon the chiefs. Commissions of inquiry, some resultant depositions, tighter government control over the appointment of chiefs and the revenue they handled, all such measures persuaded them that political activity was dangerous. By 1960 the C.P.P. had, to all intents and purposes, a monopoly over political activity, and the chiefs had little opportunity to interfere. Though chiefs may retain more local influence in Ghana than in Guinea or Mali, it cannot be said that traditional authority is any longer of political significance there.

Differences

It has been seen how the economic and social change initiated by colonial rule in both French and British West Africa brought a new group of men to the fore in indigenous society, and that it was this group which led the nationalist movements inheriting power at independence. The process of the securing and consolidation of power by this new political *élite* involved relationships with the traditional political and religious *élite*, and here certain differences between countries have been set out. It is not sufficient, however, to list differences solely in terms of the nature of the relationship; this does not tell us *why* in three of these countries – Guinea, Mali, and Ghana – the traditional *élite* has been brought far further under the control of the modern than in any of the others. Until a great deal more research has been done, it is in fact impossible to give more than the most tentative explanation of this, yet some significant evidence is to be found in studying the formation of the modern *élite*. In each of the three territories the group which gained control of the nationalist movement was marked by ideas of a radical, 'levelling' kind, often influenced directly or indirectly by Marxism. In Guinea the R.D.A. was kept alive during its difficult days at the end of the 1940s by Sékou Touré and his followers, young men, with comparatively little formal education, often experienced in trade union work, austere, with their strongest intellectual influence that of Marxism. Exploiting Touré's connexion with Samōri, and appealing to the democratic aspects of Islam, they were able to build up a devoted mass following and an impressive party organization which would tolerate no rival. Similarly in Mali the R.D.A. section there was kept alive by a devoted band grouped round Mamadou Konaté and Modibo

59

Keita, trade union leaders, ex-servicemen, and Dioula traders, again appealing to the memory of *al-hājj* 'Umar and even to that of the thirteenth-century emperor of Mali, Sundiata Keita, from whom Modibo claimed descent. In Ghana the Islamic factor is missing, but there is still the phenomenon of young, comparatively ill-educated men, often ex-servicemen or trade unionists, some of whom took their ideas from Marxist writings. These were the backbone of the C.P.P., the 'veranda boys' so despised by the Creole *élite* which they replaced.

If there was any single factor which was decisive in marking off these three *élite* groups from others in West Africa it was probably their education. For it is misleading to speak of 'modern education' as if it were a uniform experience to which all who managed to attend school were subjected. Only a few of the educated minority were able to secure university or even secondary education, the former usually in law or medicine. In consequence some of them filled the top posts open to Africans, posts which became more numerous during the last years of colonial rule. Others used their independent positions as lawyers or doctors to lead the nationalist movement itself, usually in alliance with the merchants, transporters, and contractors who had appeared as part of the process of social and economic change. Such was the typical pattern in southern Cameroun, southern Nigeria, Dahomey, Togo, the Ivory Coast, Sierra Leone, Gambia, and Senegal, where a *modus vivendi* with the chiefs was reached by the men who now form the political *élite* but are not completely cut off from the traditional setting from which their modern education had lifted them. In Guinea, Ghana, and Mali, however, it was not this group which led the nationalist movement and inherited power when the colonial system came to an end. It was, as a result of factors which scholars have only just begun to study, the less well educated, those filling the lesser posts open to the literate, whom special circumstances – among them a more uncompromising outlook, greater cohesion in adversity, and a closer relationship with the masses – gave the opportunity to take control. Nor must it be forgotten that in Guinea and Mali, though not in Ghana, the better-educated and more wealthy were fewer in numbers and therefore less dominant than in places like the Ivory Coast or southern Nigeria. In the struggle between rival heirs it was the individual circumstances of each territory which determined the winner.

Similarities

Thus far differences among the various *élites* have been emphasized. It is important, however, to conclude this survey on a different note, to stress rather the similarity of the positions in which all the political *élites* of the new states of West Africa find themselves. Products of the social change brought about by colonialism, they have inherited power from Britain and France. Few in numbers, sensitive to criticism, often suspicious of 'neo-colonialism', the members of these *élites* are at once far from and close to their illiterate relations who still live within the context of traditional society. The demands upon them are great; those of kinship and traditional obligation on the one hand, and on the other the need to use their newly-acquired power in order to change the ancient conditions of life. There is a great desire for 'development' in West Africa, a longing for better things which fostered the will to independence. From Mauritania to Cameroun it is now the new ruling *élite* which is expected to achieve this development, this improvement in the conditions of life.

3 National Unity and the Opposition

The 'heirs to the throne' did not inherit a clean slate at independence. They took over particular structures of central and local government, systems of law and education. They assumed responsibility for the direction of economies which had been developed in particular ways to meet particular demands during the colonial period. The first few years after independence were marked by the attempt to gain full control of this inheritance, and more especially to use the structures of government to tackle the problems of economic development. In the process, however, these structures have been substantially modified.

The Nation
Perhaps the most enduring legacy of the colonial period – apart from economic structure – has been the frontiers of the new states themselves. It has been frequently pointed out that these were arbitrary lines drawn upon the map of West Africa in a way which suited the Powers but which took no account of settlement patterns or ethnic ties. There were few colonial boundaries which did not cut across peoples in this way. In two cases, as we have seen, such divisions gave rise to agitation for reunification, and in one case – that of Cameroun – this was successful. On the whole, however, these frontiers have been unquestioningly accepted, first by the nationalist movements and then by the new governments after independence. Considering the bitterness with which the 'balkanization' of Africa has been denounced, indeed, it is worth considering why the division of West Africa into so many small states has been accepted by most political leaders as likely to remain for many

years to come.* (Size is taken here as a product of both geographical extent and population; thus Mali is bigger than Nigeria, itself a very large country, but has only an estimated 3,824,000 people.) A few reasons for this may tentatively be suggested.

First of all, it would appear that usage has in most cases sanctioned these frontiers, even though they have often been in existence for less than two generations. Except where border posts had actually been set up, they were not an impediment to travel in the colonial period. Admittedly French might be the official language on one side and English on the other, and different administrative and legal systems might exist side by side, divided only by an imaginary line, but this did not affect the ordinary peasant, who did not speak the official language and whose native tongue was spoken on either side of the border. Modern administration and justice were remote from his daily life and best to be avoided, since contact with them usually meant inconvenience of one sort or another. Thus, except for people like the Ewe, whose new political *élite* set out to arouse mass support for the ending of such a division, there was no great popular sentiment in favour of frontier revision as a part of independence.

It was the nationalist parties which could have associated these two demands, but in the main they chose not to do so, and that is the second reason why the old colonial frontiers have been accepted by the new independent states. The political *élite* which led the nationalist movement set itself a geographically limited objective – to capture control of the government with which it was most familiar, and that government was the territorial government. Unlike the ordinary peasant, the *élite* was interested in administrative and judicial systems, and if these were established on a territorial basis, then they became the target of nationalist struggle. In so far as the C.P.P. was trying to gain control of the structure of government in the Gold Coast, its interests stopped short at the territorial frontiers, and its sympathy for other nationalist movements was the very general 'ideological' one of sympathy for all resistance to

* A further discussion of attitudes to African unity will be found in Chapter 7.

colonialism. In French West Africa the most prominent nationalist party, the R.D.A., and other parties as well, were admittedly established on an inter-territorial basis. Nevertheless, closer examination soon shows that in fact the R.D.A. was based upon three strong territorial sections, those in the Ivory Coast, Guinea, and Soudan. Moreover, after the elections of March 1957, governmental power began to pass to the sections, and not to the R.D.A. as a whole. Interests came into conflict, so that by the end of 1958 the Guinea section had left the party altogether, while that of Soudan was negotiating with the R.D.A.'s old rival, Léopold Senghor, for the formation of the Mali federation.

The melancholy history of that short-lived federation provides a third reason why the old frontiers have not been subjected to a process of revision. The creation of the new Mali was a conscious attempt to create a larger, stronger, richer unit which would be in a better position to negotiate with France and develop its own resources. As has been seen in Chapter 2, however, different political *élites* have evolved in different circumstances, and developed their own special interests. When the crucial moment came, the majority of the *élite* in Upper Volta and Dahomey was not prepared to take the risk of submerging itself in a larger unit, even a federal one; it preferred to join the Entente Council a little later, an act which did not involve the wiping out of frontiers and the merging of political systems. Senegal and Soudan were left to go it alone, and even they parted after eighteen months. Once again the *élites* which had come to power in these two territories found that their interests and outlooks were opposed, and that it was easier for each to work separately within its own frontiers.

The political *élites* in the new states have found it easier to work within the frontiers inherited from the colonial Powers because it is within these that they have full control of governmental power. At a time when there is an almost universal desire for social and economic change, this is not surprising, since for such change power is all-important, and at the moment of independence power could only be gained within the framework of the old colonial frontiers. This is the fourth, and indeed the most important, reason for their preservation. The colonial governments were only prepared to hand over power on a territorial basis, within the frontiers that they themselves had once drawn on the map. It has even been alleged of France that, when this process was begun by the *Loi Cadre* reforms of 1956–7, power was deliberately 'territorialized' in order to weaken African unity. The British, of course, never really envisaged any alternative to an individual evolution towards independence. Whatever the underlying motives, the colonial Powers bequeathed their inheritances – naturally enough – within the already-established frontiers, and the prospect of power overrode what few objections there might have been to such a condition.

This acceptance by the modern leaders of the old colonial divisions as the material basis of their political power, whatever the talk of 'balkanization' and 'African unity', has made West African nationalism a somewhat unusual phenomenon. Like earlier nationalist movements in Ireland or Poland, it has been primarily and understandably a reaction against foreign rule, seeking above all to restore the dignity of people who felt themselves degraded by centuries of exploitation and control. Yet the vision of the nationalist movement was not expressed in terms of a 'nation state', of making West African political units coterminous with pre-existing cultural unities. As we have just seen, the new states manifestly do not coincide with ethnic boundaries, and with few exceptions there seems to be little desire to make them do so. The approach of the West African nationalist leaders has tended to be an empirical one, devoted to the winning of power in whatever context it could be gained, rather than to theorizing about the nature of the Nation and the State. One of the leading nationalists, Kwame Nkrumah, for instance, makes no real conceptual distinction in his many writings and speeches between 'state', 'nation', and 'country'; he uses the terms interchangeably.[1] Nationalist writings in general have not emphasized the existence of nations prior to the colonial period with a right to self-determination. The references to the ancient empires of Ghana, Mali, and Songhai are intended to refute the charge that Africans have no history and no culture, rather than to prove the historical existence of nations which have a right to be sovereign states. Modern Ghana is not even geographically the same as ancient Ghana, modern Mali covers only part of the area of ancient Mali, and as yet there is no modern Songhai. Indeed, if a nation is conceived as having a common culture, language, and historical experience, as the eighteenth- and nineteenth-century European writers held, then the closest approximation to national sentiment in West Africa must be the 'tribalism' so often denounced by the nationalists. Léopold Senghor has gone half-way to recognizing this, but prefers to call such an entity the 'Fatherland' (*Patrie*). In a speech given at the constituent congress of the P.F.A. on 1 July 1959, he defined this as

... the heritage which our ancestors have passed down to us. One soil, one blood, one language, at least one dialect, manners, customs, a folklore, an art, a culture rooted in a land and expressed by a race ... In West Africa, the Fatherland is the country of the Serer, Malinke, Songhai, Mossi, Baoulé, Fon.[2]

Thus if nations do not exist in West Africa, if each of the modern states, like Dahomey or Sierra Leone, is in fact a collection of 'Fatherlands', it is necessary to establish nations. Once again, this has been recognized by Senghor. Speaking of the Nation in the same speech, he declared:

It is not, like the Fatherland, a natural phenomenon, therefore an expression of its surroundings, but rather of a will to construct, better, to reconstruct. It is, objectively, a *restructuration* in the image of a given model, an archetype. But in order to attain its object the Nation must animate with its own faith all its members, all individuals, passing beyond the Fatherlands. From individuals it must make persons, that is to say conscious wills, souls. ... It will unite the values of the Fatherlands, or, more often, choose among them those which, because of climate and the history of the race have a common denominator or a universal value. When it is realized, the Nation makes a harmonious whole out of different provinces; a single country for a single people, animated by the same faith and directed towards the same goal.[3]

If then a West African nation has consciously to be constructed, it is likely to come into being *after* independence, when the power to do so has passed into the hands of the nationalists, rather than before. The new leaders have bent themselves, though not always as consciously as Senghor, to this task. Speeches and articles constantly stress the importance of unity and attack 'tribalism'. Emphasis is laid upon the symbols of national unity, flags, mottoes, and anthems. In some countries the Head of State himself is so treated, President Nkrumah's position in Ghana being the most highly developed example of this.

In some instances an attempt is being made to create a 'myth', upon which loyalties can be focused and around which the new nation can be built. In Guinea or Ghana it is 'the Revolution' which is the national myth. In Senegal this phenomenon is of more than usual interest. There the breakdown of the Mali Federation on 20 August 1960, the failure of an attempt actually to transcend the colonial frontiers, is being made part of the 'myth' of Senegalese independence. Commenting upon the formal inauguration of the Federation on 4 April 1959, and upon its dissolution on 20 August 1960, a Special Independence Celebrations Number of *Senegal Magazine* had this to say:

In the life of a country how many wars and revolutions does one not count? However, there are few October 17s, few 14 July 1789s. These historic moments are chosen among many others because they comprise aspirations often decided upon on the spot, but continually renewed across the centuries. They serve thus as reference points and crystallize around them the 'Myth of the Fatherland' or symbolize the human ideal of the nation in question. Senegal is no exception to the rule. Certainly on 4 April our people did not go to put flowers upon the tombs of the Martyrs of a 'bloody revolution' which the wisdom of the colonizer and the political sense of our leaders allowed us to forgo. Is this to say that we are incapable of taking 'Bastilles'? The night of 20 August is there to bear witness to the sacrifices which the children of this country are able to accept in the name of Liberty and Independence.[4]

Even in the possible absence of certain objective conditions for the formation of a nation, therefore, the new *élite* has the will to create one, and tries to inculcate this will into everyone. Mamadou Dia, writing on 'Towards a New Definition of a Nation', defined it as

... an affirmation, a perpetual movement, an unfinished construction ... one might define the nation as a collective vocation, depending on a common scale of values, common institutions, and, finally, common aims.[5]

In this view, nations are to be willed into existence, as independence was willed; the nation, in fact, becomes the 'daily plebiscite' of Ernest Renan, whom Dia cites approvingly in the passage quoted above.

Unity

With this emphasis upon the need consciously to construct new nations, it is scarcely surprising that great stress should be laid upon the need for unity in the years immediately after independence. The new rulers inherited not only particular structures of government from the colonial period, but also the political situations which had developed during the last decade of British or French rule. In these last years the new modern *élite* had not existed as a monolithic bloc, united and of one opinion only. Even the unifying force of the nationalist movement had not always been able to transcend personal, ideological, or ethnic rivalries, and as the prospect of power became less and less remote, these had come to the fore. Sometimes, too, the traditional *élite* had grown alarmed for its future after independence and tried to swing its weight against the potential heirs to the throne. In each territory the nationalist party had had its rivals – in the French colonies they had often been encouraged by the administration – and these, though commanding less support, nevertheless constituted an inherited problem to be faced.

Three main trends developed in response to this challenge, trends which in some instances became apparent several years before the actual date of independence. First of all, the new *élite* showed itself increasingly hostile to participation by Africans from other territories in the politics and administration of its own territory. Secondly, there was a tendency for parties and other bodies – especially trade unions and youth movements – to unite within individual territories and sever their connexion with organizations seeking to span several.

Lastly, and most important of all, opposition parties and leaders not voluntarily joining the party which succeeded the colonial administration found themselves subject to coercion of one sort or another. These trends may be examined in turn.

Theoretically, and practically for certain economic and administrative purposes, French West Africa had been treated as a single unit. People travelled freely between territories, and often lived and worked for long periods, sometimes the whole of their working lives, in territories of which they were not natives. This was especially true of civil servants, many of whom came originally from Dahomey and Senegal, but by no means exclusively. A man from Soudan could become a political leader in Niger, could even be elected to the Territorial Assembly there and become a minister. In British West Africa links between territories were much less close, despite the existence of bodies like the West African Currency Board or the West African Institute of Social and Economic Research. Nevertheless, Nigerians might live and work for many years in the Gold Coast, and natives of the Gold Coast in Nigeria, while Creoles from Freetown were to be found in every territory, often holding the highest positions open to Africans. Political leaders were far less mobile, but there is a famous example in the case of Dr Azikiwe, who became the editor of a newspaper in Accra after his return from the U.S.A. in the 1930s and only returned later to live permanently in his native Nigeria.

At times the colonial administrations took steps to deport unwelcome outsiders. Thus in October 1956 the Governor of Sierra Leone ordered an estimated 30–50,000 'foreign strangers' living in the diamond-mining areas to leave the territory within three weeks. This was an attempt to restore law and order in an area where diamonds valued by some sources at £18,000,000 had been illicitly mined and smuggled out of the country. As control has passed into the hands of African leaders, they have been quick to follow the example of their predecessors, refusing to tolerate the 'interference' of strangers in what they now consider to be their own preserves. Association with opposition parties has brought retribution to some, like the Nigerian leaders of the Moslem Association Party expelled from Ghana after independence in 1957. In French-speaking Africa leading political figures have found their extra-territorial origins a handicap during an internal party dispute: Abdoulaye Diallo was forced to leave the Council of Government in Soudan and return to his native Guinea in 1958 after opposing the decision of his colleagues to vote 'Yes' in the de Gaulle referendum. A reversal of colonial practice has been the tendency to send home civil servants who have been working in other territories. Thus the replacement of Dahomeyans by Senegalese necessitated a visit by Hubert Maga to Dakar at the end of 1959, and when the Southern Cameroons federated with Cameroun in October 1961 Nigerian civil servants there found it necessary to leave. Interestingly enough, the same process has taken place even inside the Federation of Nigeria, with southerners in the public service of the Northern Region being replaced by northerners and forced to return home in increasing numbers from about 1957 onwards.

If the years immediately before and after independence have seen the new states to some extent turn in on themselves, this process has been matched by the efforts to secure internal unity. This tendency, however, has been far more marked in the French-speaking than in the English-speaking countries. In the former, part of the great debate which broke out after the *Loi Cadre* reforms was concerned with the issue of the *parti unique* (single party) or *parti unifié* (unified party): whether the dominant party might in any way be justified in extinguishing the others or whether all ought to seek union as a new party representative of all interests. As was seen in Chapter 1, the proposed union on an inter-territorial level between the R.D.A., M.S.A., and Convention Africaine failed to materialize early in 1958, but the process of unification was by that time already launched within the various territories. In June 1956 a number of youth groups in the Soudan merged, and this process was repeated in Guinea and the Ivory Coast in May and July 1957. The tendency also manifested itself at the same time in the political parties: in August 1956 Senghor's B.D.S. agreed with two minor Senegalese parties and some individual members of the local R.D.A. section to merge into the new Bloc Populaire

Sénégalais. African organizations, it was felt, should put more concerted pressure on the colonial power in order to secure further concessions, and as power began to pass to them the tendency became more marked. In some territories the decisive factor was the existence of one particular party as the clear and only possible successor to the colonial administration. Thus in Guinea the opposition P.R.A. had merged with the P.D.G. by the end of 1958. In the Soudan the smaller parties all merged with the Union Soudanaise–R.D.A. during 1959. Elsewhere the process was rather more prolonged, as a number of parties similar in strength struggled to be heir to the throne. In Dahomey Hubert Maga's rise to power was partly due to the merger of his northern-based R.D.D. with the southern Parti des National- istes du Dahomey in November 1960. Mauritania offers another example, with its four parties (one of them by then technically illegal) moving together between May and December 1961 to form the Parti du Peuple.

This tendency to unification with the approach or attainment of independence was found not only among political parties, but also among youth groups and trade unions, naturally enough considering the close connexion of these with the parties. In- deed, the attainment of power by one party and the use of its new position to put pressure on these other organizations has often been decisive. Part of the same process, as noted earlier, has been the severing by these organizations of their links with inter-territorial movements like U.G.T.A.N. (Union Générale des Travailleurs d'Afrique Noire, see page 32), a sign of the growing conflict of interests between groups of West African states. Thus in July 1960 the majority of the unions in Upper Volta formed a 'National Union', while similar bodies were formed in Mauritania and Senegal in January 1961, and in Dahomey in February. In a similar way unified 'national' youth organizations have replaced the diverse groups of pre- independence days. In July 1962, for example, the Constituent General Assembly of the National Union of Senegalese Youth was held, attended by delegates from the youth movement of the governing U.P.S. and representatives of youth clubs, the Boy Scouts, sports associations, and similar groups. It was decided to set up a National Council and coordinating committees at all levels, and it was recommended that young people be interchanged between administrative Regions and urban and rural areas, and that a special 'Secretary for the Training of Cadres' be appointed. The emphasis was thus upon the role of youth in fostering national unity, a key-note struck by the Minister of Youth and Sports in his opening address:

You felt that for our under-developed states certain independences would be dangerous. That is why, rising above all difficulties, leaving behind the quarrels of your elders, you have decided on the creation of the National Union of Youth of Senegal, which will be another tool for the building of a Senegal always engaged in the struggle for a free and prosperous Africa.

In English-speaking West Africa this tendency to unification has not been so apparent, for the development of parliamentary institutions in the years before independence encouraged the parties in opposition to think of themselves as potential alternative governments. In Nigeria each of the major parties was entrenched in a particular Region, and each hoped to be the ultimate heir to the throne. In the Gold Coast the various opposition parties, which joined to form the United Party in October 1957, hoped up to the eve of independence to secure a federal constitution which would protect their interests. Only in Sierra Leone was there a move towards unification with the establishment of the 'United National Front' in March 1960, in preparation for the forthcoming constitutional talks. In May a coalition government was formed, and by April 1961, the month of independence, most of the previous opposition leaders had joined the S.L.P.P. A potentially important new opposition party had come into existence, however, in the form of the All People's Congress, led by the former trade union leader, Siaka Stevens.

Similarly, in much of English-speaking West Africa trade unions and youth groups have tended to remain diverse and divided. Once again this is, of course, related to the situation of the political parties, to which many of the unions and youth groups are formally or informally linked. In Nigeria a long dispute culminated in the formation of the rival United Labour

Congress and Independent United Labour Congress in May 1962, and although the Federal Government has recognized the former as the official spokesman of Nigerian labour, there has been no attempt to force the creation of a 'national' organization, closely linked to the government, such as is to be found in the former French territories. A like picture of diversity is to be found among youth groups, with party organizations existing alongside those of the Boy Scouts, the churches, and similar bodies. In Sierra Leone the picture is also one of continuing diversity. Only in Ghana is the situation markedly different. The trade unions there were closely linked to the C.P.P. from the beginning, and in January 1958 the Fourteenth Annual Convention of the Trades Union Congress endorsed a proposed new structure, which made the organization in effect a government agency for the management of labour relations. By mid 1963 moves had also been made to integrate the various youth organizations with the party.

The Opposition

However strong the formal or informal pressures which have resulted in voluntary and peaceful merging of parties and other organizations in the name of national unity, in many countries the most significant factor has been the deliberate use of its power by the governing party to destroy the opposition. In a few instances the years immediately before, and in many instances those immediately after independence have been marked by the imprisonment of opposition leaders and the banning of their parties. There were, of course, many precedents for this in colonial practice, and the African leaders showed no hesitation in following the examples that had been set them.

The C.P.P. government in Ghana paved the way in the years immediately after independence. Kwame Nkrumah and his administration had displayed a remarkably conciliatory spirit in the period 1954–7, when the C.P.P. was for the first time being strongly challenged by opposing parties. The attainment of independence in March 1957, always Nkrumah's top priority, however, left him free to deal with his opponents as he wished. Constitutional guarantees were in no way proof against a

73

C.P.P. majority in the National Assembly. Foreigners involved in politics were deported, religious, tribal, and regional parties made illegal, and hostile chiefs deposed. Party militants were appointed as Regional and District Commissioners. The Preventive Detention Act of July 1958 gave the government the power to detain anyone for up to five years without trial. The final step followed the report, in May 1959, of the Granville Sharp Commission of Inquiry. This unanimously found the United Party General Secretary and another of its leaders guilty of conspiracy 'to carry out at some future date in Ghana an act for an unlawful purpose, revolutionary in character'.[6] Two of the three commissioners also believed that there had been a conspiracy to murder Kwame Nkrumah. The report was decisive, because it now associated the United Party not with 'legitimate' opposition but with sedition. The party continued to be legal, but defections from its ranks and the detention of its leaders gave it only a token existence.

In French-speaking West Africa this tendency has also been marked, especially where the struggle between rival heirs to the throne has been prolonged and bitter. Elsewhere, in territories which had been dominated by one party all along, without an effective challenger, the process was rather one of absorption, as seen above, than of suppression. This was the pattern in Guinea, Soudan, and the Ivory Coast. In Senegal Senghor's party has remained dominant throughout, but has reacted to criticisms from the left by banning the Marxist Parti Africain de l'Indépendance and imprisoning its leaders. In Upper Volta, Niger, Dahomey, Cameroun, Mauritania, and Togo, the period from the end of 1959 until early 1962 – and in some instances even later – saw a struggle for power which involved the use of governmental authority to ban rival parties and imprison their leaders. Hubert Maga's consolidation of his position in Dahomey, for example, involved the adoption in February 1961 of a new Public Security Law – allowing the detention of persons 'whose activities endanger public order and security, the credit of the State, or manifestly tend to compromise the setting up of the Republic of Dahomey' – and also a new Press law. Armed with these the government moved. In April a series of Presidential and ministerial decrees dissolved the chief opposition party and the local trade union organization affiliated to U.G.T.A.N. and suspended the opposition newspaper *Cotonou Matin*. In May opposition leaders were accused of plotting and arrested, and in December the most prominent of these was sentenced to five years imprisonment by a Special Criminal Court. With slight variations, this is the pattern that has been followed in the other countries listed.

Although Ghana led the way among the formerly British territories of West Africa, Sierra Leone and Nigeria did not lag too far behind. In Sierra Leone, the strong criticism by Siaka Stevens of the negotiations leading up to independence and his attempt to force elections before it was actually granted, together with his obvious appeal to the more radically-minded young men, caused the government to declare a State of Emergency on the eve of independence. Stevens and other leaders of the All People's Congress were detained for a few weeks, and in June 1961 Stevens was sentenced to six months imprisonment on charges of sedition, conspiracy, and libel. His party has not been banned, and the measures taken in Sierra Leone are markedly milder than those in Ghana or the French-speaking states. Nevertheless, Sir Milton Margai's government has shown that it is quite willing to take measures against the opposition if it considers them necessary, and the trend of events is likely to reinforce this tendency. A slow rate of economic development and growing radicalism among the youth could finally damn the opposition in the eyes of the governing party.

In Nigeria the existence of three strong regionally-based parties since 1951 has given the impression that a viable opposition existed, at least at the federal level, but appearances have been deceptive. Although the election of December 1959 resulted in a coalition federal government formed by the N.P.C. and the N.C.N.C., with the Action Group as the official Opposition, it cannot be said that the last was ever potentially an alternative government. Mustering only seventy-five seats out of 312 at its strongest, it was never allowed by the government to behave as the Opposition is expected to behave in following the Westminster model.[7] In May 1962 the frustration felt by the party's leaders resulted in an internal split, weakening its hold over the government of the Western Region, which had not been affected by its defeat in 1959. The federal government thereupon assumed direct control of the West under a State of Emergency, and instituted an inquiry into the Action Group's handling of the Region's finances. Many Action Group leaders were detained, and others took refuge abroad. In November Chief Awolowo, the party's President, and a number of its other leaders and organizers were put on trial for sedition and conspiracy to overthrow the government.

Liberia, the other English-speaking independent state, has followed a pattern all its own. There the Whig or True Whig Party has remained continuously in power since 1860, except for a short period during the 1870s. In the twentieth century it has never had a serious rival, though it has nevertheless found it necessary to use the power of the government against individuals regarded as potentially dangerous.

The tendency for the opposition to disappear, or at least for its existence to be threatened, seems to be universal throughout West Africa. The reasons, however, are not arbitrary ones. The absence of effective oppositions and the intolerance shown by governing parties towards other ones stem from fundamental characteristics of the new states at their present stage of development. Of first importance is the absence of social divisions which might form a basis for rival parties. Social classes such as exist in industrial societies are only just beginning to form, and then only in the towns, so that there is as yet no basis for a Marxist clash of interests. 'Business' and 'labour' interests are not yet well-developed enough to form the nucleus of competing parties with different programmes. The only deeply-rooted rival interests are those of different ethnic groups, and though these have frequently nourished at any rate minor parties, such 'tribalism' is abhorred by most West African leaders, who are determined to eradicate it. Moreover, 'tribalism' could never by its very nature throw up a party which could behave as an alternative government. The only real division in the new states is perhaps that between the government and the governed, though this is in some ways a false antithesis, since if these interests ever seriously clashed, it would be a sign that the whole political system was breaking down. Furthermore, such an antithesis could not form the basis of a working party system, since the government is something which theoretically all should have an equal chance to control. It is the very fact of the monopoly of governmental power and authority by one party which makes it difficult for any rival to survive. In the circumstances it is easier for members of the *élite* to give up their rivalries and for all to claim a share in this power, since there are, in any event, too few of them at present to necessitate a serious competition for places.

These sociological factors are reinforced by the basic attitudes of the politically aware. In the new states of West Africa the emphasis is on development, on the raising of living standards among the masses from whom the new governments derive their legitimacy. In face of this the constant emphasis is upon unity and concerted effort. Consensus of opinion is valued, partly because this has always been so in traditional African society, but more especially under modern conditions because dispute seems to hamper the tackling of huge and pressing problems. There are no real ideological divisions, no disputes over ends, since all are agreed that the end to be attained is development like that of the industrial countries. If there is a genuine dispute at all, it is merely over the means to this end, and in such a situation the ideal role of the opposition is to act as an informed and intelligent critic of government policy. This is recognized in theory by the West African leaders, but they allege that the criticism offered is ignorant and unintelligent instead, actively harmful rather than useful. As Léopold Senghor has said of the opposition:

> Its role is certainly to criticize. But criticism is the critical spirit, not the spirit of criticism, systematic denigration.[8]

The case was stated perhaps even more clearly by the Ivory Coast's Minister for National Education in 1959, when he wrote:

> Certain people say that in the Ivory Coast it is not possible to set up

opposition parties. You cannot write what you wish. That is futile. In our Republic we have never thrown men into cells because they have expressed their ideas. The Prime Minister has said several times that the Republic would permit an opposition on condition that it was intelligent and constructive. That is to say that the government of the Ivory Coast defends all individual liberties of conscience, economic and political liberties. . . . But true liberty is not anarchy, as certain people would wish, but the precise and objective determination of the interests of all.[9]

When measured against this ideal, the opposition is universally judged to be wanting, sometimes with reason. Faced with the task of building a nation, of uniting the disunited, and of raising the living standards of all, the ruling party is thus prone to deal harshly with its opponents. Moreover, political power is desirable in itself, and the ruling party is loath to see its monopoly threatened. In these circumstances all West African governments can only agree with the reported remark of the Chief Justice of Sierra Leone, when passing sentence upon Siaka Stevens: 'I am afraid you, the restless people, must be checked.'

The Concentration of Power

The process to be seen at work in the new states, therefore, in some cases immediately before, and in all cases immediately after independence, is the concentration of political power in the hands of the leaders of one dominant party. The essential distinction between colonial status and independence is the location of this power; with independence it passes from the colonial rulers to their nationalist heirs. In not every instance was it immediately apparent which group of the *élite* would finally inherit this power, but in any struggle the decisive moment usually came when one group secured a firm enough control over the machinery of government to use its authority against its rivals.

In a situation where the *élite* is expected to get things done, and where only the power of the State can do them, such power becomes the ultimate prize, to be shared with no one. As has already been seen, this means that all rival parties must be absorbed or destroyed. It also means that no other organization, or even social group, can be permitted to have an independent existence if this implies a threat to the governing party's monopoly of power. We have noted some ways in which trade unions and youth groups have been affected by this attitude. To complete this chapter some further consideration must be given to these, as well as to the position of civil servants and the Churches.

What then is the objection of the governing party to these organizations? Simply this, that if they are permitted to retain interests independent of those of the party, the interests may sooner or later become opposed and clash. The interests of civil servants are not always identical with those of the politicians, whose policies they are supposed to implement. Trade unions in theory exist to protect the interests of their members, and in these countries the governments are the single most important employers of labour. The objection to youth groups is that young people, and especially students, are more prone to radical ideas than their elders, more ready to criticize and demand a rapid rate of social and economic change. Youth groups contain a high proportion of the 'restless people' (as indeed do the trade unions), potential critics of the new governments. Lastly, the Churches claim an exclusive sphere of influence – the souls of men – which for centuries has brought them into conflict with the State, and this is as true of modern West Africa as any other area at any other time.

These potential conflicts of interest have not always become actual, but the politicians have been aware of them, and in most instances have taken steps to bring possible rivals firmly under control. Thus the unions and youth groups have not only been tempted and cajoled to form 'national' bodies closely controlled by the government in the name of unity, they have also been openly threatened, and, where necessary, action has been taken against some of their members. In May 1960 Senghor warned trade unionists to forsake politics and confine their attention to more limited spheres:

Despite its past services, because of these services, trade unionism today must transform itself again by formulating for itself a more precise idea of its own role and its tasks. Because there are today well-organized political parties, which on the level of general policy represent the whole Nation, trade unionism must revert to its natural role, which is, above all, to defend the purchasing power of its members.[10]

In fact, trade unions in West Africa have not even been allowed to retain this, their traditional role. More and more the new national unions are becoming government agencies, no longer concerned with making bargains over wages and working conditions but instead expected to increase productivity, maintain labour discipline, and help workers newly arrived from the rural areas to adjust to the problems of town life.[11] Those forgetting their new role and attempting to revert to the old one have often been sternly admonished. In May 1961 the Union Nationale des Travailleurs du Niger passed a series of resolutions demanding, among other things, a revision of the labour code, a rise in the level of family allowances, and 'the intensification of the struggle against big business by the effective control of prices'. The answer of the Political Bureau of the governing party was to denounce this as the work of 'irresponsible and ill-informed elements', and to reprove 'all the excess of language and the use of outdated slogans which risk compromising the struggle for economic independence'.

Youth has fared no differently. In French-speaking West Africa it was at one time felt that the growing numbers of young men with degrees and other qualifications (there were 2,957 government scholarship-holders in the 'professional' and 'higher' categories during 1957) might swing the political balance when they returned to their homes, imbued as they were with radical, often Marxist, ideas.[12] In August 1959 the students of Upper Volta were holding their fourth congress, and the usual militant and critical speeches were being made, when on the last day the head of the government, Maurice Yaméogo, unexpectedly arrived and addressed the students.

If I am here today it is not in my capacity as President of the Council, for you do not deserve to have a President of the Council leave his seat for you. If I am here, it is to replace the Minister of National Education, who has been prevented from coming. During the whole of this conference you have behaved like spoiled children. I was perfectly well aware what was said every day upon this platform, but I have held back and allowed this congress to go on to its end to prove first that democracy is not an empty word in Upper Volta, then to know exactly what is biting you. I have this to say to you: you have amused yourselves nicely, you have spat well on everybody, but now the fun and games are over, for your brothers of the Volta labour daily to pay for your studies and not to launch you upon a criminal enterprise of demolition. Even if you have discovered the word liberty you do not yet know what it means, you take your ideas from the newspaper *L'Humanité* [the French Communist newspaper – *author*], you are soaked in everything which cannot be said to men, for you are only children. I will not take your insults; if you have no self-respect at least respect your elders.[13]

Words have not failed to be supplemented with actions. Two courses, for instance, were adopted by the government of the Ivory Coast. On the one hand, special efforts were made in the elections of April 1959 to find Assembly seats for prominent members of the youth section of the governing party, who had recently criticized its leadership. On the other, not long after the incident in Upper Volta described above, the Ivory Coast dissolved the association of Ivory Coast Students in France, and replaced it with a 'National Union' which was more closely under control. In July 1961 eight students expelled from France because of their left-wing activities were imprisoned on their return to the Ivory Coast. In January 1962 it was announced that they would be released, provided that they acknowledged the sole authority of the National Union. This example could be paralleled elsewhere in the French-speaking countries, and it would appear that the dominant *élite* has not found it too difficult to curb the potentially radical influence of recent graduates and in general to bring the youth under control.

In the English-speaking countries the tendency towards tight control is less advanced. Students studying abroad have generally had less close contact with Communist and other left-wing organizations. In Ghana radical attitudes can find means of expression through the dominant party itself, though students in Ghana's own universities have tended to be somewhat conservative and politically quiescent. Their counterparts in Nigeria have on occasion been politically active, as in November

1960, when they demonstrated against the Anglo-Nigerian defence pact, but they have never constituted a serious threat to the dominant parties, which control most sources of employment for the young men when they graduate. There is, however, a growing number of young people leaving the schools and failing to find work (see Chapter 6), and this may force the Nigerian parties to take more definite steps in the future. The same will in time probably prove true in Sierra Leone. Liberia's government is unlikely to have to take any extensive measures to bring the youth under control in the near future, since there is a very low level of education in the hinterland and the few graduates can be absorbed into jobs quite easily.

The civil servants and the Churches have caused the dominant parties in the new states less trouble than the trade unions or youth. The former are a less well-articulated group than the unions, and less radical than the youth, as well as being disinclined to make public pronouncements upon matters of policy. Nevertheless, civil servants can wield a great deal of indirect influence upon events, as the more intelligent politicians realize. They are also capable of developing a group-consciousness through the existence of professional associations or even social clubs (the Nigerian Federal Ministry of Finance and the Central Bank, for instance, have their own social club, known as 'MinFin'). In a number of countries, also, where an old Creole *élite* has lost its dominant position to a newer modern *élite*, members of it have continued to occupy many senior positions in the administration: such would certainly appear to be the case in Senegal and Ghana. As a consequence of all this the political leaders find it necessary on occasion to remind the civil servants of their duty to obey. Thus, at the congress of the U.P.S. held in February 1962, Senghor announced in his speech that the salaries of Senegalese civil servants were to be cut as an austerity measure, and in the speech of Ousman N'Gom, the party's Political Secretary, it was ominously remarked that the relations between the party and certain civil servants left something to be desired. Senegal is, in fact, one of the few countries where the conflict has ever become open. Before independence, at the end of 1958, administrative reorganization following the establishment of the Franco-African Community had necessitated dismissal of a number of civil servants. On 28 November there was a sudden strike of administrative workers in Dakar, and another in Thiès shortly after. A decree issued on 5 January 1959 allowed the dismissal of any administrative employee who went on strike in contravention of the Labour Code, and another four days later provided for the drafting of civil servants if necessary. By April the government felt strong enough to re-employ all those who had gone on strike, provided they had not disturbed the public peace. Since then warnings such as N'Gom's have sufficed. Nevertheless, in Senegal as elsewhere, the potentialities for a clash of interests still exist.

The last of the potential rivals to the governing parties, in the sense at least of providing an alternative focus of loyalty, is the Churches. Not only do they claim a dominion all their own, but the most important of them also have overseas connexions, since they were originally established by European missionaries. In the circumstances, therefore, remembering that strong nationalist movements seeking independence have only recently accomplished success, the Churches have tended to tread delicately. Yet, in three of the states of West Africa, there have already been serious clashes with the government. The first took place in Guinea during August 1961, when the French Archbishop of Conakry was expelled after he had protested against a decision by a conference of the P.D.G. to integrate all private schools into the public system. The conference had also criticized the failure of the Roman Catholic Church to 'Africanize' the clergy. The Archbishop had then made the classic statement that the church 'is and will always remain entirely independent from all temporal power', but in fact the integration of the schools was ultimately accepted, and an Archbishop appointed who was an African, though not a Guinean. The clash in Cameroun during February 1962 resulted from the death by suffocation of twenty-five political prisoners while being moved by train. This was reported first in a Catholic weekly; the government's reaction was to seize the issue and two days later to order the editor, a European priest, to leave the country.

The third instance involved the government of Ghana and the Anglican Church there. Early in 1962 the Minister of Education announced, after a tour of schools, that he had noticed 'disquieting signs in a number of missionary institutions, signs of subtle but manifest disloyalty to the ideas of the state'. In August the Bishop of Accra and the Archbishop of West Africa (both Europeans) were expelled from Ghana, the first for criticizing the C.P.P.'s Young Pioneer movement, the second for supporting him. Both were subsequently allowed to return, but the point had been made, as it had in Guinea and Cameroun. The governments of the new states will not tolerate any act or pronouncement by the Churches which suggests that they feel their interests to be opposed to those of the State. In this the Churches are regarded as at one with the unions, youth, and the civil service.

Stability and Uniformity

It can now be seen that one of the first objectives of a governing party in West Africa has been to foster a sense of national unity, and to do this primarily by drawing all political power into its own hands, leaving no other organization capable of materially influencing government policy. Despite variations, more markedly perhaps between countries of French and English-speaking West Africa, this tendency can be observed frequently enough to describe it as general. In this way the new political *élite* has been united under one banner, with only a very few articulate dissidents, mainly now in gaol. Some of the deep-lying reasons for this have been examined, but it is only fair to remark in conclusion that this apparent stability, this absence of fundamental dispute over ends and means, has been bought at the price of a uniformity which may prove dangerous. In suppressing the opposition, in associating it with sedition and conspiracy, the dominant parties in various states have denied such of their opponents as are still at liberty any means of expressing themselves *except* through violence. It cannot be denied that opposition politicians in West Africa have plotted in the past, have condoned the use of violence. The present situation, however, leaves them with no other alternative. It may be that this desire

NATIONAL UNITY AND THE OPPOSITION

for uniformity, for a government monopoly over all forms of power and influence, is inevitable in the early years of independence, possibly even desirable. Its effect upon the long-term stability of the new states may prove unfortunate.

85

4 The Institutions of Government

By the beginning of 1963 there were only five states in which
there were still opposition parties – Cameroun, Senegal,
Ghana, Nigeria, and Sierra Leone – and in the first three these
were of little significance. Not only was there a general absence
of effective organized opposition, but there was an absence of
'countervailing powers' of any kind. Power was concentrated
as a monopoly of one party, not distributed between it and a
number of other organized interests. Although we may discard
any rigid theory of 'checks and balances', it may be suggested
that in a modern representative political system there is at least
a fairly equal opportunity for any organized interest to bring
pressure to bear upon the government. In such a system these
interest groups enjoy an independent existence. This is not so
in West Africa, where in all but a few states such interest
groups as consciously exist have been brought firmly under the
control of the governing party. Some of these were discussed in
the previous chapter, but this characteristic is equally true of
others – women, farmers, members of cooperative movements,
and such entrepreneurs as may exist. Thus in Ghana the trade
union, youth, women's, and farmers' cooperative organizations
are all officially regarded as 'wings' of the Convention People's
Party. In such states, where the dominant party is highly
organized, the only way in which these different interests may
make their views felt is through the machinery of the party.
In fact the party more often uses them to make the government's
policy acceptable to the people, as when the United Ghana
Farmers' Council Cooperatives are used to deduct the six
shillings from the price of each load of cocoa which is the farmers'

contribution to the National Savings Scheme. In other states the party may not be so well organized, and the various interests may find that they have no regular means of making their views known.

It seems safe to assume that this situation was neither intended nor envisaged by the retiring colonial Powers. Britain in particular set out to create 'Westminster' systems of government, developing the necessary institutions slowly in the course of the last decade of her rule. France's case was more complex. Such basic democratic principles as the freedom of the Press were frequently flouted by the government in France itself during the last years of the Fourth Republic, while the constitutions of the African states, first of all as members of the Community and then as independent entities, were drawn up in the shadow of General de Gaulle and his new Fifth Republic. This latter point must be examined later. Suffice it to say now that the great body of liberal opinion in France as in Britain can hardly have expected such a rapid or complete centralization of power in the new African states as in fact has occurred.

Nevertheless it has occurred, and in a very short time after independence. The institutions established during the last few years of colonial rule have been drastically modified, sometimes in form, frequently in the role that they play in the political system. Legislatures, Councils of Ministers, local government structures are none of them now what the former colonial Power thought that they should be. Two main reasons may be suggested for this. First of all, the dominant party has asserted its complete control over these institutions, making them virtually adjuncts of itself. This is the phenomenon referred to by Mamadou Dia as 'The Indispensable Symbiosis of Party and Government'.

The moment has come finally to transcend former oppositions between the governmental and political apparatuses. We must recognize with courage and clarity that in this sphere there are too many tenacious old reflexes in us which plunge their slender roots far down into the colonial epoch. It is no longer possible to have a divergence between the party and the government, or the government and the assembly.[1]

The second reason for the rapid and radical transformation of institutions after independence is possibly more deep-rooted in basic attitudes towards the political system as a whole. In some other societies, such institutions have a recognized legitimacy of their own, a legitimacy often hallowed by time and usage. Usually they pre-date the parties which at present compete for their control, so that the parties to some degree derive their own legitimacy from these institutions. This, however, is not the case in West Africa. The dominant party usually came into existence before the institutions which were written into the independence constitution. The party has a monopoly of political legitimacy, as it has of political power, and it asserts – by time and usage – an exclusive claim to the support of 'the People'. Moreover, it is generally more acceptable and readily understood, because the institutions of government are associated in men's minds with the former colonial administration. It is, in fact, the party which legitimizes the institutions by accepting them at the moment of independence, and in doing so asserts its right to deal with them thereafter as it thinks fit. As a result therefore, the constitution may be amended, or even replaced altogether by another, not long after independence. Thus in Ghana the C.P.P. began by amending the constitution of 1957 in order to make it a more convenient instrument, and ended by adopting another, of a very different nature, in 1960. Each of the French-speaking countries adopted a new constitution at the time of its independence. Though such constitutions may have retained certain already existing institutions – assemblies, councils of government, supreme courts, and the rest – the roles envisaged for these in the future may be quite different from those which British and French constitutional lawyers intended at the time when these bodies were planted in West Africa.

'The Indispensable Symbiosis'

With the monopoly of power held by a single party, the pattern of institutional development immediately after independence is not difficult to understand. The party has asserted its control over all the organs of government, legislature, executive, judiciary, and local administration. It has even gone beyond this.

It does not recognize any distinction between 'public administration' and 'politics', that a problem can be approached on
more than one level. Problems of government are seen as
problems of power, which are the particular province of the
party, not as questions of law and administrative procedure.
Thus it is not recognized that there can be any independent
administrative point of view, since the party, as the representative of the People, must always be right. This is in part a
reflection of the former colonial situation, where there was no
real distinction between the administrative and the political.
Policy was both formulated (admittedly under the general
control of Colonial Ministers) and implemented by the same
people – the Governor and his subordinate officials. Moreover,
their only legitimacy was the right of conquest and the claim
to have a 'civilizing mission'. Considering the basic simplicity
of this situation, it is easy to understand why the new African
rulers should feel no necessity to evolve or adopt some highly
intricate division of powers. Thus, the absence of a balance
of power in the political system is matched by an absence of constitutional checks and balances. The independence of the judiciary is also often in doubt; in some countries – Senegal and the
Ivory Coast, for instance – special courts, made up wholly or in
part of politicians, have been set up to judge 'crimes against the
State'. In this situation two tendencies have become evident:
first, for the executive authority to dominate all others, and
secondly for the distinction between party and government
rapidly to disappear, in the roles that they play in the political
system and even in their structures.

A number of commentators have remarked upon the tendency
towards 'presidentialism' in the new states of West Africa,
more especially in the French-speaking ones.[2] By this is meant
the tendency not merely for the executive to exert a moral
authority over the other arms, but for the President, as both
Head of State and Head of the Government, to possess over-
riding powers. As was remarked earlier, this is scarcely surprising
when it is remembered that their constitutions were evolved at
a time when France, their institutional model, had passed under
the rule of General de Gaulle, and in doing so had adopted a

new constitution which itself much increased the relative powers of the President. Nevertheless, the trend has much deeper sociological and political roots than a mere tendency to imitation, and this is proved by the fact that the most sweeping powers of any West African President are those contained in the new republican constitution of an English-speaking country, Ghana, which came into force on 1 July 1960.

Adoption of a republican constitution does not necessarily imply a move towards presidentialism. Nigeria's adoption of a republican constitution in October 1963, three years after independence, merely confirmed that for the English-speaking states the British constitutional tradition mattered less than the apparent indignity of retaining the British monarch as their Head of State, and the President is really just the old Governor-General under a new name, with a Prime Minister as chief executive. Nigeria, however, has the special problem of satisfying both dominant parties, and the obvious unwillingness of either of them to see a powerful presidency in the hands of its rival has necessitated this more carefully balanced system. The example of Senegal illustrates the more typical trend in West Africa. From 1960 to 1963 the importance in the U.P.S. leadership of two figures, Léopold Senghor and Mamadou Dia, necessitated that one of them should be President of the Senegalese Republic, and the other, President of the Council of Ministers. Then, in December 1962, the final battle for political supremacy was fought between them, with Senghor emerging victorious and putting his rival under arrest. The new constitution, adopted after a referendum held in March 1963, merged the two sets of powers in the office of President of the Republic. Thus Senegal after some hesitation finally followed the trail blazed by the other French-speaking republics, by Liberia, and by Ghana.

The overall picture would appear to suggest, then, that with few exceptions the trend is for one man in each state to be elevated to a position of great power. In every instance he is the dominant figure in the governing political party – Félix Houphouët-Boigny in the Ivory Coast, Kwame Nkrumah in Ghana, Maurice Yaméogo in Upper Volta, Sékou Touré in

Guinea. The constitution reflects this domination of the state not only by a single party but, within that party, by a single man. Thus, in the four Entente states – the Ivory Coast, Dahomey, Niger, and Upper Volta – which have virtually identical constitutions, the President is the exclusive holder of executive power. He alone appoints and dismisses ministers, he alone makes all civil service and military appointments. Proposed laws may be referred back to the National Assembly by him, and then require not merely a simple but a two-thirds majority of all members to be passed again. The Assembly can delay the approval of the budget for only seventy days, after which period it is put into effect by decree. If the President wishes, any matter may be referred direct to the people by referendum, though he must have the agreement of the Bureau of the Assembly. Votes of censure on his government require a two-thirds majority, and in Niger and the Ivory Coast may not be brought at all during the first three years of the government's five year term of office. In Ghana, too, the President is both Head of State and chief executive, and his powers are equal to, and in some cases greater than, those of the Presidents in the Entente states. He has an outright veto upon all legislation, for instance, and it is specifically stated that he need take the advice of no one. Moreover, Part X of the constitution, which was added after the draft had been approved in the plebiscite of April 1960, bestows upon the first President (already named as Kwame Nkrumah in Part III) the power to give directions by legislative instrument 'whenever he considers it to be in the national interest', and to alter any enactment other than the constitution.

Ghana, in fact, provides a very clear example of how power has been concentrated in the hands of the President, not merely by the provisions of the constitution but also because as chief executive he has consciously sought such concentration. Dr Nkrumah is, of course, supreme within the governing party, its Life Chairman and since May 1961 its General Secretary, and Chairman and Secretary of its Central Committee. He has assumed direct control over the vitally important fields of finance and economic development through the Bureau of the Budget, the State Planning Commission, and the State Control

Commission. In April 1961 he became Chairman of the Board of the new Volta River Authority, responsible for the most important single item in the development programme. By mid 1963 the President was directly responsible for twenty-four separate subjects. With their growing importance in the administration of the country, the President's Office and staff had become an increasingly important item in the Ghana budget – £6,885,080 in 1961–2 and £9,798,010 in 1962–3.

Ghana's example may be particularly clear, but it is unusual only in the degree to which the executive has become dominant. The same general trend is visible throughout West Africa, and was apparent even in the English-speaking states before they became republics. In Nigeria, where the theory of parliamentary government would suggest the ultimate control of the legislature over the executive, the role of the former was changing fast during the years 1960 to 1963. The legislature existed for two main purposes, first to set a formal seal upon the legislation which the government desired, and secondly to act as a forum where local interests might be expressed by members, who sought to secure as large a share of development projects for their own constituencies as possible. This was true of both the federal and the regional legislatures. As a result, sessions were short; the Federal House of Representatives met for only forty-four days in 1960, fifty-four in 1961, and forty-two in 1962. Formal divisions for voting upon bills were few, and members did not exploit fully their right to put questions. Perhaps most important of all, the financial control of the legislature – historically a central issue in the development of parliamentary democracy – persistently diminished.[3] The major check upon the federal government increasingly appeared to be no longer the established procedures and powers of parliament but the need for political compromise between the two partners in the coalition government. This became even more obvious when the workings of the regional Houses of Assembly were examined, since in two of these at least – the Eastern and Northern – the party in power faced an even smaller and more ineffectual opposition. This trend has in no way been changed under a republican constitution. The sole element lacking in Nigeria is the national dominance of a single party, and the absence of this is almost fortuitously linked with the emergence of a federal political system in the country.

The growing importance of the executive in West Africa represents the gradual concentration of power into the hands of a few party leaders, a process made possible because the party itself is dominant, and often indeed the only legal one in existence. As a result, the politics appear on the surface to be much less complex in these states than in the 'developed' countries. Attention need be focused only upon the party, or rather upon its leaders. Without the manifold pressures of opposing forces and an elaborate body of constitutional theory and administrative precedent, institutions have little life of their own. Party central committees appear more important than cabinets, party congresses rival legislatures, and party branches supplement or even replace local administrations. Important government decisions are openly made not by Councils of Ministers, who may or may not be members of the party's central committee, but by sessions of the central committee itself. This was explicitly recognized by Modibo Keita, now President of Mali, and the nature of the relationship between party and government defined, in a speech delivered at a conference of party 'cadres' in May 1960:

... we wish to say that the elaboration of a determined line of conduct, in no matter what sphere, and the choice of solution which will be decided on, reverts in the final place, after necessary advice and information received at all levels, to the Political Bureau of the Union Soudanaise–R.D.A. It is the Party which sets a seal on the directives to be given to such and such an activity, but it is the Government which is charged with the execution.[4]

Thus the seventeen members of the National Political Bureau of the Union Soudanaise–R.D.A. meet in the party's headquarters every week to determine policy. It was they who decided in February 1961, for instance, to recognize the F.L.N.'s Provisional Government and the Gizenga administration in Stanleyville as the legitimate governments of Algeria and the Congo (Léopoldville) respectively. Important issues are, for the most part, debated more thoroughly – and critically – at party conferences in West Africa than in legislatures. Thus in Guinea it was conferences of the P.D.G. which decided in February 1960 to introduce the new Guinean franc and in August 1961 to adopt a policy of 'positive neutralism' in foreign affairs, to reform education, and to rationalize working methods. This pivotal role of party assemblies is unconsciously, or perhaps even consciously realized, so that the formal opening of such conferences becomes a more important state occasion than the opening of a legislative session. All the panoply of the State – bands, parades, and guards of honour – is produced to adorn what in the British view at least is a party political event.

This open identification of party and government at the upper levels, as well as in local administration, has gone furthest in the 'radical' countries – Ghana, Guinea, and Mali. Nevertheless, it is doubtful whether the leaders of dominant parties anywhere, even in the states where a multi-party system still exists, would disagree with Modibo Keita's formulation:

> In order that our political action should be more and more effective we must always tend to the improvement and the reinforcement of the cooperation between the Political and the Administrative. Henceforward the Administration is the emanation of the Party. Party, Elected Body, and Administration unite in the same goal: liberation of the people, the fight against poverty and ignorance, organization of production, national construction in peace and unity. Legislative Assembly, Government and administrative machine overlap and interpenetrate one another.[5]

Governing parties everywhere in West Africa can discern no real difference between their own interests and those of the State as such, whether in using public funds for party purposes or employing local administrations for the harrying of opponents. On this, such very different parties as the Action Group and the Northern People's Congress in Nigeria, the Parti Démocratique de la Côte d'Ivoire and the Parti Démocratique de Guinée are agreed. They differ not in their basic attitudes to the political process but rather in their style of action, which is itself dependent upon the social context within which they work. Thus the P.D.G. and N.P.C. can both regard local administrative structures as instruments to be used in the party's interest, even though these structures are very different in their respective areas of control and the social forces behind the parties are themselves quite incompatible. The degree to which the party has been able to assert its control of administrative procedures has also depended upon the type of governmental structure it has inherited from the colonial power. Here the centralizing tendencies of the French, and their less vigorous insistence upon a division between the administrative and the political, has made the task easier in their former possessions than in those of the British. This would account for some of the differences between Guinea and Ghana, whose governing parties are comparable in their radical approach and the efficiency of their organization. But organizational questions can also determine the extent and nature of the control by the party over administrative structures. There is a difference between the governing parties in Guinea and the Ivory Coast, though both the states are former French colonies. The latter's P.D.C.I. lacks the highly developed local party structure which the former's P.D.G. uses to reinforce its control of administrative personnel. This sort of factor may be observed much more easily at the level of local administration than can the 'symbiosis' between the party and the institutions of the central government, and it would be useful at this point to extend the scope of our examination to all levels of government.

Local Administration and the Party

In whatever manner decisions are taken at the centre, it is at the local level that they have to be implemented, and it is there that they have their detailed impact upon the everyday lives of the citizens. Most people derive their picture of the government from its conduct at this level – arbitrary or representative, efficient or bungling, 'for us' or 'against us'. It is accordingly at this basic level that policy is likely to determine whether people are generally satisfied or dissatisfied with their new rulers. The government views the popular contacts of its representatives at this level as providing the best source of information about the 'Will of the People' which it claims to represent. Moreover, activity in the localities is constantly growing as development plans are put into operation. Yet it is this level which generally constitutes the weakest part of the administrative structure, the one most vulnerable to corruption and with the fewest well-trained and experienced officials, so that there is a tendency for the new rulers to fall back on the instrument they know best – their own parties. Party militants may be used as administrative personnel, and party and administrative structures brought closer together. In some states the party even assumes administrative functions.

Three sets of protagonists, then, may be discerned in the localities. First of all there are the agents of the central government – the administrative officers, heirs to the colonial district officers or *commandants de cercle* and directly responsible to the Ministry of the Interior or of Local Government, and the technical officers responsible to other ministries. Secondly there are elected local councils, also responsible to the Ministries of the Interior or Local Government, but possessing certain executive powers distinct from those of their direct agents and claiming a second responsibility – that to the electors. Lastly there is the local organization of the governing party, inevitably connected with the second set of protagonists, since the party in general controls the local council, but also, of course, having an independent existence. All three in fact 'overlap and interpenetrate' – to use Modibo Keita's phrase – and it is the varying nature of this relationship which concerns us here.

Once again, an important factor in determining this relationship has been the colonial heritage, and once again this heritage was different in French and English-speaking West Africa. Just as the British set out during the last decade of their rule to build up a system of parliamentary central government, so they also sought to establish a system of elected, responsible local councils. Indeed, it was regarded as desirable to promote local councils as a foundation of experience in elective government upon which parliamentary institutions could be built. Thus elected councils were introduced in Eastern Nigeria during 1950 and in the Gold Coast during 1951, while it was the new Action Group government which itself initiated this reform in Western Nigeria during 1952. Sierra Leone lagged behind in this as in its constitutional development. The District Councils in the Protectorate were not given any executive authority at all until 1950, and the first elections to them were only held in 1956. In Northern Nigeria a pragmatic policy was adopted, with elective elements gradually introduced into Native Authority Councils after 1951, so that by the end of 1961 slightly less than half of them had elected majorities. Throughout British West Africa party rivalries, inefficiency, and corruption retarded the development of the system. The nationalists, while regarding these reforms as desirable because of their 'democratic' nature, in fact successfully concentrated their efforts upon winning control of the central government. The foundation for parliamentary government, theoretically regarded as essential, was in practice never fully laid.

The French in their possessions were less concerned with elective local government, preferring to rely on direct rule by the administrative officers, sometimes in collaboration with the local chiefs, who might or might not be traditional rulers. For many years it was only in certain urban 'communes' that there was any elective local government, and in 1955 there were only three of these – Saint Louis, Rufisque, and Dakar, all in Senegal – which had both an elected council and an elected mayor. A further thirty-five possessed elected councils and an administrative officer as mayor, while eighteen had merely nominated councils.[6] In the rural areas there were Councils of Notables, but they were only advisory. Then, in November of the same year, a new local government law gave fully elected councils and mayors to all the communes. The *Loi Cadre* reforms envisaged the establishment of councils for 'rural collectivities', but by this time African leaders were acquiring a measure of control over territorial governments and were able to influence developments. Thus in both Guinea and Senegal reforms of local administration were carried out in the latter part of 1957. It was upon the structure of central government, however, that the African leaders concentrated their attention, and elected councils were never developed in French West Africa to the same extent as in the British territories.

This difference in historical development has been one of the main factors determining the different approaches to local administration in the new states of West Africa. In the French-speaking countries the central government has continued to rely upon its own agents to carry the main burden of local administration. As the Senegalese Minister of the Interior put it when discussing the administrative reforms of 1960:

> The Government has, in fact, preferred to retain the French administrative formula, which centralizes in the hands of a prefect the complete range of administrative powers, rather than adopt the English solution, for example, which does not contemplate this centralization.[7]

French commandants have been replaced by African, but their responsibilities have remained much the same, or even been increased. The system of elected local councils has been extended, both on a regional and a village level, in Senegal, Mali, and Guinea for instance, but the actual powers of these councils have remained limited. In Dahomey it was even announced in January 1962 that the former communes were to be renamed 'urban circumscriptions' and administered in future by sub-prefects, like other circumscriptions, with nominated instead of elected councils.

The situation in the English-speaking states is rather more complex, for there the system of elected local councils with well-defined responsibilities, though never developed to its fullest extent – important powers remained in the hands of local administrative officers at the time of independence – has nevertheless created a vested interest which must be taken into account. Many of the most active members of the governing party are involved in such councils, and derive much of their local influence from their membership of them. Yet the councils are often corrupt and inefficient, and are sometimes controlled by a party opposed to the government. In these circumstances there has been a growing tendency since independence for central governments to create new posts which will be held by reliable party men able to exercise a close watch over local affairs. This was done in Eastern Nigeria in 1959 and Northern Nigeria in 1962, with 'Provincial Commissioners' appointed in each instance, while in Sierra Leone 'Resident Ministers' were appointed to the Provinces in 1961. Not only have new posts been created, but as in the former French territories existing administrative officers have been brought under party control. Thus in Ghana after independence expatriate Regional and District Commissioners were rapidly replaced by party stalwarts. In Nigeria and Sierra Leone the young Africans who are replacing the expatriate administrative officers are still career civil servants, but it naturally behoves them to cooperate closely and amicably with the party in power. And so in English- as in French-speaking West Africa, there is a growing tendency for local administration to become 'politicized', either by the creation of parallel offices or by the assertion of party control over previously existing ones.

A more detailed examination of the administrative structure in two different areas will help to illustrate some of the problems involved. Senegal may be used to illustrate what might be called the 'French' tradition of administration, and Western Nigeria the 'British'.

In Senegal the structure of local administration was remodelled in 1960, with the objects as in a number of other French-speaking states, of establishing a system better able to serve the demands of economic development. Thus the Région du Fleuve was created in October 1958 as part of the first pilot development scheme. A new law passed in January 1960 created seven Regions in all, Cap Vert, Thiès, Diourbel, Fleuve, Eastern Senegal, Sine-Saloum, and Casamance. These were then further divided into twenty-eight *cercles* and eighty-five *arrondissements* – the old colonial system of 139 *cantons* now disappeared – with each *arrondissement* grouping together 15–35,000 people. Such were the rural divisions, and in addition some thirty communes existed as urban units of local administration, with a total population exceeding 600,000 – over a third of them in the capital, Dakar, itself – out of Senegal's almost 3,000,000 people. The communes were to be ruled by elected muncipal councils and mayors, while in charge of each rural Region was a Governor, aided by two Deputy Governors, one of whom was specially charged with responsibility for economic development. The Governors were not themselves to have powers of decision, but instructions were to come direct from the various ministries to the commandants in charge of the *cercles*, though the Governors were, of course, to be kept informed. The role of the Governor was to preserve an overall control and to coordinate the activities of the commandants, to act indeed as regional inspector of the administration. He was to be a 'permanent envoy of the central power to those who carry out policy, and a permanent envoy of those who carry out policy to the central power'.[8] The actual implementation of policy was to be the responsibility of the *commandants de cercle*, who were to be 'the mainspring of governmental action'.[9] Subordinate to them were the *chefs d'arrondissement*, of great importance because they were to be the representatives of the central government who actually came into daily contact with the ordinary citizens. About fifty of those appointed in 1960 were former *chefs de canton*, but it was stressed that they were henceforth to regard themselves as civil servants, possessing no traditional connexions with their areas and transferable at will.

Along with an attempt to adapt the administrative structure to suit the needs of development, there was a certain measure of decentralization. A law of 1 February 1960 provided for the establishment of regional assemblies, elected by the universal suffrage of rural voters; the communes did not take part. These were to have some budgetary powers – subject to the approval of the Ministry of Finance – involving expenditure on such matters as schools, dispensaries, and public works, and were also to concern themselves with investment in their region, again under the control of the central authority responsible for the development plan. Although this was a notably 'democratic' change from French colonial practice, the powers granted to the assemblies were not, in fact, substantial; the biggest regional budget in 1962 was that for Sine-Saloum, 227,402,000 C.F.A. francs, while the national budget for the year was 36,145,246,568 francs. The government in Dakar continued to rely in the main upon its own agents for the direct administration of the rural areas. Governors, commandants, and *chefs*, as well as mayors in the communes, continued to play a role which was both political and administrative. The struggle for power between Senghor and Dia in December 1962 accordingly involved a demand by Senghor for a written assurance of loyalty from Governors and commandants, and four Governors and thirteen commandants were relieved of their posts when they failed to comply. With a governing party that was frequently admitted to be *'pas bien structuré'* (not well organized) in the localities, administration in Senegal depended to a considerable extent upon the direct agents of the Ministry of the Interior, whose incumbent was heavily involved in the crisis at the end of 1962.

In Western Nigeria there may be found another tradition of local administration at work, one which attempts to combine the political and the administrative in a different way, by giving the latter functions to an elected body. The first important piece of legislation introduced by the new Action Group regional government in 1952 (local government in Nigeria is a regional matter) was a Local Government Act, by which a 'three-tier' system of elected councils was set up, with powers distributed among Local, District, and Divisional Councils. The powers of these bodies, in matters such as education, health, local roads, and markets, were extensive, and the authority enjoyed by the direct agents of the regional government was correspondingly reduced. Following the passing into law of a further Local Government Bill in 1957, administrative officers were in fact restyled Local Government Advisers, though they also continued to act as government inspectors.

The system has never worked as well as was hoped. The first problem has been that of sheer inefficiency. The three-tier system itself soon proved unwieldy, and since 1957 there has been a move towards the establishment of a two-tier system, with the removal of Divisional Councils, so that the original 226 bodies have been reduced to about 160. The greatest single handicap has been the difficulty of finding honest and efficient permanent staff and councillors. There have been some notable scandals – such as those revealed by the inquiry into the Ibadan District Council in 1956 – and significantly, in the last few years, the government has been driven to dissolve some councils and replace them by Sole Administrators. The most important instance of intervention was the replacement of the Abeokuta

Urban District Council by one of the few expatriate non-technical officers still in the Region's service; during his period of administration in 1962–3, he turned a financial deficit of £45,000 into a £14,000 surplus.

The other basic problem has been the effect of politics upon the conduct of local government. As has been noted, a great deal of political influence in Nigeria is derived from control of local councils, and the party in power has not hesitated to use its position in order to further such control. Thus in Western Nigeria the number of 'traditional' – as opposed to elected – members, which is restricted by law to a third of the total but need not be as high as this, has sometimes been increased to the maximum in order to ensure a majority for the governing party. The weapon of dissolution has also frequently been used, with the pretext of inefficiency and corruption ever at hand. It is not without significance that, when the State of Emergency in the Region ended on 1 January 1963, the Minister of Local Government and Deputy Premier in the N.C.N.C.–United People's Party coalition which had replaced the government of the Action Group, should have felt it necessary as one of his first tasks to tour various areas and examine the local councils. Early in February twenty-five councils were dissolved by the new government at a single stroke, with all but one area placed under the sole administration of the relevant Local Government Adviser. In the following months further councils were dissolved.

Three years after independence it was apparent that, although the system of local government councils was more highly developed in Western Nigeria than in any of the other Regions, no satisfactory balance had yet been struck there between direct administration by representatives of the central government and the wielding of important powers by elected councils. As has already been remarked, there is a clear trend in the other Regions of Nigeria, in Ghana, and in Sierra Leone, towards the appointment of administrators who are also politicians to keep an eye on local affairs. The local council system will no doubt continue to exist both in these areas and in the Western Region, but a further shift of emphasis towards the Senegalese system of direct, centralized control is not at all unlikely.

In order to complete this discussion of the three elements in local administration – administrative officers, local councils, and party structures – an example must be given of a system in which the party manifestly plays the most active role. It is in the 'radical' states, Ghana, Guinea, and Mali, that the dominant party is best organized to do this. Ghana, however, has inherited the system of elected councils, and although the C.P.P. controls every one of these, the nature of the system makes the party's participation in local government rather less direct than in the other two states. The process has perhaps gone furthest in Guinea, where the P.D.G. local committees have themselves assumed an administrative function and are even responsible for the registration of births, marriages, and deaths. At the 'Congress of Truth' held in Conakry at the end of December 1962 President Sékou Touré even envisaged the complete replacement of elected village councils by village party committees. Nevertheless, it is Mali which will be taken as an example here.

In his speech to the Conference of Party Cadres in May 1960, already quoted, Modibo Keita announced a reform of the administrative system. Six Regions were established, corresponding to the economic areas delimited for planning purposes, and these were subdivided into forty-two *cercles* and 179 *arrondissements*. Thirteen of these *arrondissements* were communes, five of them autonomous, with elected councils and mayors, while fifteen others, made up of 'Nomadic Tribes and Fractions', were left under their traditional chiefs but given elected councils. At the head of each Region was a Governor, charged with the execution of policy as well as the overall control and coordination of his subordinate officers, the *commandants de cercle*, and the *chefs d'arrondissement*. These were the main executives of policy, and at the lowest level there were *chefs de village*, responsible for law and order and such matters as the maintenance of local roads and bridges and public hygiene. There were elected councils for each village, *arrondissement*, *cercle*, and Region, and though these were in the main advisory, the Regional Assemblies – as in Senegal – had certain financial powers. They voted the annual regional budget, and had to be consulted by the Governor on taxes levied in the Region and on economic and social development projects there.

Thus far the picture is not very different from that in Senegal, except for the existence of elected councils at all levels, and it must be remembered that the two systems were conceived at a time when Mali – then known as Soudan – was joined together with Senegal in the Mali Federation. The distinguishing feature of Soudan then – as of Mali now – was the existence of a militant and highly-organized ruling party, the Union Soudanaise–R.D.A. By 1960 it represented the totality of political life in Soudan. As Modibo Keita put it in his speech:

> The members of thirteen Municipal Councils and thousands of Village Councils and smaller units are its militants. The Government is its emanation. The *Chefs de circonscription* are equally militants delegated into administrative functions. In our present position, the Party dominates everything, organizes and directs the country.[10]

The party has accordingly been in a position to control the activities of the administration in two ways. First of all, the administrative officers themselves have been party militants, empowered by a decision of the party's Directory Committee to attend the meetings of local party committees in their areas – a step 'which avoids misunderstandings, incomprehensions, and makes work easier and more effective in an atmosphere of confidence and free comradeship'.[11] Secondly, the party itself and its parallel youth and women's wings have been well enough organized to dominate the elected councils and to maintain a constant contact with the officials. Mamadou Dia's 'indispensible symbiosis' has been carried right down to the level of the villages.

Procedures and Hierarchies

Early in this chapter we noted a tendency in the West African states to draw no firm distinction between the administrative and the political. There is nothing wrong in this, of course; it violates no code of institutional ethics. Indeed, it has been shown that there are good and sufficient reasons why the new rulers should regard the political as supreme. Nevertheless, writers on bureaucracy from Max Weber onwards have stressed the importance of certain prerequisites in public administration. These may be conveniently reduced to two essentials: the existence of an established procedure for dealing with a problem, and the existence of an established hierarchy of responsibility for decisions. No system of administration can work efficiently unless it meets these essential preconditions, and as the demands upon the administration grow – in the West African context, as development plans get under way – the need for efficiency will grow too. Yet particularly in those countries in which the governing party is well-organized, there is a grave danger that the line between what the party should do and what the administration should undertake will become so blurred that no one will know what procedures to follow or who takes which decision.

Two examples may suffice, a minor one from Ghana, a more serious one from Guinea. In Ghana the President in 1962 made a present of much-needed textbooks to secondary schools. This involved no political consideration. Yet at least one of the schools which benefited wrote its letter of thanks not to the President's Office, or even to the Ministry of Education, but to the acting Administrative Secretary of the Convention People's Party, asking him to convey its gratitude to the President. In Guinea President Sékou Touré found it necessary to circularize regional commandants and their subordinates and heads of technical departments in May 1960 over 'a grave lapse in administrative discipline'. A subordinate administrative officer had sent his monthly report direct to the President, instead of forwarding it through his immediate superior.[12] These examples could doubtless be repeated many times.

What may finally be suggested, then, is that parties and administrative systems have different roles to play in achieving the same goal. Even though the party may determine policy, even though the symbiosis between it and the central legislature and executive may be far advanced, the problem of how to execute policy at a lower level still remains. In the next chapter the phenomenon of 'mobilization' for economic development will be discussed. It is this which the party can do, and no other institution. Its contacts with the people, its militancy, and its experience of campaigning make it particulary suited to the task of arousing popular enthusiasm for some necessary government measure. The administrative implementation of this measure, however, requires different qualities. Method, precision, regularity are the key words here. Working closely together party and administration can accomplish much, but neither is fitted to do the work of the other. In Senegal, where the local work of 'cadres' in popularizing development schemes would appear to be a task for which the party would be eminently well-suited, these men are in fact usually local teachers recruited by the Ministry of Technical Education and the Training of Cadres. Where the discipline and dynamism of a well-organized party are lacking and such key figures are paid employees, it is all too easy to dissipate energies in squabbles over such bureaucratic details as the rate of travel allowances. Conversely, party zealots may have to be reminded that an administrator's insistence on method need not necessarily indicate lack of enthusiasm. As Modibo Keita put it:

... The circle commandants, who are in almost every case approved militants, have a sense of responsibility at least as developed as that of numerous political bureaux of sub-sections. The role of political bureaux of sub-sections or of elected members is not to put themselves in the place of the executive power but on the contrary to support it in its actions.[13]

It is significant that in Guinea, the country where the process of symbiosis has progressed farthest at all levels, there is a growing awareness among the political leaders of the need to preserve some distinction between the role of the party and that of the administration. Thus, although local administrators may attend meetings of party committees in their areas, it was laid down after the Labé Conference of December 1961 that they might not themselves assume political responsibilities at this level. Following the 'Congress of Truth' in December 1962, which was concerned with the future role of the party, a redistribution of portfolios and State Secretaryships left only four of these in the hands of members of the party's National Political Bureau. Previously, twelve of its seventeen members had been Ministers or State Secretaries. It is, of course, impossible to estimate how far and how consistently this attempt to separate the party structure from both the central government and the local administration will be carried in years to come. Certain other features of the Congress – discussion on the role of village committees, for instance – seem to suggest an empirical approach rather than an overall policy. In Guinea and throughout West Africa, the basic structures of government are still being evolved as part of the response to the new fact of political independence. The governing party, as the architect of this independence, asserts its claim to absolute control. It remains to be seen what form the institutions of government will take when the balance between the demands of administrative efficiency and this political assertion is finally struck.

5 Economic Development

The concentration of power in the hands of the governing parties of West Africa and the remodelling of institutions to suit their purposes is occasioned by something more than the simple desire of the ruling *élite* to eliminate all opposition. There is everywhere a great sense of urgency, a desire for rapid change, particularly economic and social change. The period of nationalist struggle made not only the leaders but many of their followers aware of the poverty and disease so widespread in their countries. In those states where the concept of the Revolution is part of the new national myth, it is often suggested that there are in fact two Revolutions – the first, the nationalist movement against the colonial Power; the second, the one 'which heralds the coming of a bright new era for all, a revolution destined to transform radically and completely the entire face of our beloved nation and our human society'.[1] In a speech given at a C.P.P. rally on 1 May 1961, Kwame Nkrumah himself officially announced the end of the internal political revolution in Ghana and the beginning of the new revolution, directed to the liberation of all Africa and the economic development of Ghana. In West Africa the governing party feels itself under constant pressure to demonstrate the superiority of its rule compared with that of Britain and France, and in this situation, as Madeira Keita of Mali has put it,

The sole aspiration, the sole will which inspires us is that of finding the means of putting a state apparatus at the service of economic, social, and cultural development.[2]

The C.P.P. of Ghana has put the point even more plainly:

Socialism can be achieved only by a rapid change in the socio-economic structure of the country. To effect this, it is absolutely essential to have a strong, stable, firm, and highly-centralized government. This means that power must be concentrated in the country's leadership.[3]

Finally, Kwame Nkrumah has emphasized not only the need for the concentration of power but also for a united national effort:

As comrade delegates know, we are embarking upon a period of intensive industrialization and the mechanization and diversification of agriculture. This is the time, therefore, when we shall need every available hand. The intelligentsia, the workers, the farmers and peasants, all the people must pull together in one great effort to liquidate and abolish all the remnants of the evils of colonialism – illiteracy, disease, poverty, hunger, malnutrition, and squalor. All the people must work together, for our interests are one and inseparable and our destiny is one and single.[4]

This sense of urgency and profound desire for change may be prevalent in West Africa, but enthusiasm alone cannot break established patterns of trade or cause industries to grow. Economic development must ultimately depend upon hard economic facts. It is therefore essential to look a little more closely at the economic situation in which the new states of West Africa found themselves at the time of independence.

The Colonial Economy

Just as the boundaries of the West African territories were the creation of the colonial Powers, so also were their economies. There had been economic activity on a large scale long before the European occupation, at least in trade; the centuries-old Saharan caravan trade owed little or nothing to European enterprise; but it was the Europeans who created economic systems for each of the new West African divisions in the period after 1885, and caused each of them henceforth to look outwards to the sea. The characteristic features of this process have already been noted in Chapter 2: the establishment of direct political control by the Powers and the 'pacification' which accompanied it were the essential first steps. Before this the European traders were dependent upon the whims of the African middlemen, who could always close the trade paths if they wished. The imposition of European control, however, broke the old middlemen and gave the new rulers a direct grip on the economy. The governments provided the essential bases; law and order (paid for by the new taxes), uniform currencies, roads and railways for the easier export of cash crops and minerals. The opportunities to earn the new money and buy the new consumer goods made the African producers receptive to economic change. New crops were introduced, and new strains of old crops. New tastes for imported goods developed. A new group of middlemen appeared, partly African, partly European, and partly Levantine, moving between the farmers and the trading companies. Subsistence agriculture and traditional handicrafts still survived, and even predominated over substantial areas. Yet these were now, by common agreement, the most backward areas in each territory. It was the others which set the pace, producing the cash crops and using the consumer goods.

The economies which were thus cast in a new mould were relatively simple ones, meeting certain basic European needs. These needs were for primary products like groundnuts, cocoa, coffee, and palm oil. Even minerals were of relatively little importance before the Second World War, although they possessed some significance in British West Africa – iron ore from Sierra Leone, gold and diamonds from the Gold Coast, and tin from Northern Nigeria. The pattern was soon established. African farmers produced almost all the cash crops, for European-owned plantations were rare, kept out of the British possessions by deliberate policy, significant in French West Africa mainly in the Ivory Coast. Middlemen bought these crops and supplied imported goods; in Nigeria and the Gold Coast they were usually Africans, while in the French territories Lebanese traders and the Frenchmen themselves – either as independent operators or as company employees – were more significant. The big European trading concerns like the United Africa Company or the Compagnie Française de l'Afrique Occidentale finally bought the crops from the middlemen, to whom they also supplied imported trade goods, and exported them in ships owned by European companies in which they usually had an interest.

The bulk of trade was with the particular Power to which the territory belonged, and from the same source came most of the capital needed for mercantile and mining enterprise. Thus we may characterize the 'classical' colonial economies of West Africa as severely limited in their range of products, sources of capital and markets, and as predominantly agrarian, with production in the hands of peasant farmers.

The period after the Second World War brought some changes. The Labour Party which came to power in Britain in 1945 wished to accelerate the progress of the colonial possessions towards independence and realized the need for economic and social development as part of this progress. Successive post-war French governments were anxious to develop the Overseas Territories so that they might play a fuller part in the affairs of the French Union. Both attitudes implied a considerable increase in metropolitan investment in West Africa. British public investment was made primarily through the machinery set up by the Colonial Development and Welfare Acts of 1940 and 1945, while the French operated through the Fonds d'Investissement pour le Développement Économique et Social (Investment Fund for Economic and Social Development – known as FIDES), which originated from a law passed in April 1946. Thus in the years 1947–57 FIDES invested more capital in French West Africa – 96,000 million C.F.A. francs – than the total estimated investment from both public and private sources in the period 1903–46. In the years before the Second World War the total British capital investment in West Africa considerably exceeded that of the French, representing some 9.56 per cent of the total capital invested in Africa, compared with France's 2.49 per cent.[5] After the war, however, the position was reversed, and France invested much more heavily in West Africa than Britain. In both cases much of this investment was in road-building, but the French also invested heavily in ports and railways, and the British in hospitals and schools.

Increased investment was not the only change in British and French economic policy after 1945. In British West Africa, the Marketing Board system was developed out of a war-time expedient, designed to ensure government control over supplies of raw materials. Government boards undertook the purchase of cash crops, using the same middlemen and trading companies as the buying agents did, but replacing the latter as the channel through which these crops were exported. They also guaranteed prices, whatever the state of the world market. The prices paid for cocoa, groundnuts, and palm produce by the boards in the early and middle 1950s were lower than world prices justified, and theoretically the profits thus made were to support prices paid to farmers when world prices fell. In fact, however, these relatively large sums were used partly to swell Britain's gold and dollar reserves and partly to finance development projects in West Africa. Subsequently, as investigations into the financial Affairs of Western Nigeria in 1962 showed, they were also used to finance party activities when the political leaders gained more control over the machinery of government at the end of the colonial period.

The change in French economic policy during the years between the Second World War and the attainment of independence was in keeping with the traditional policy of centralization. French West Africa had always been treated as an economic unit, and tariff policy had been designed to give the greatest possible advantage to France, both in imports and exports. The early fifties saw a growing recognition that a more liberal attitude was necessary, and the Mendès-France government in 1954 initiated a policy of price-supports for West African products. Not only were the prices of commodities like groundnuts, cocoa, and coffee guaranteed by the French government at rates above the world level, but the territories were also assured each season of the amount of each crop which France would buy. France's response to the problems of marketing was thus not that of Britain, the creation of new local institutions, but rather a continuation in a new form of the old policy of central direction.

The changes in the French Union following the *Loi Cadre* reforms did not affect this general policy. For as long as independence was ruled out as a political solution, French West Africa could be treated as a single economic unit. Investment could be directed through FIDES and the Central Bank of Overseas France in Paris, and one currency, the C.F.A. franc, used. In mid 1957 the Ministry for Overseas France set up a permanent commission to coordinate economic relations between France and her territories. All of this was quite acceptable to the African leaders in the territories themselves. They were well content to see the French government guarantee to buy a fixed quantity of groundnuts, even when, as in the 1956–7 season, this involved it in compensating merchants for the storage and insurance of an unsaleable surplus. At the end of 1957 Ministers from Senegal, Soudan, and Niger fought hard – and successfully – to force the French government to raise both the price of groundnuts for the 1957–8 season and the amount it agreed to buy.

The period after the Second World War accordingly saw some changes in the economic policy of the two colonial Powers, but the basic nature of the West African economy was not affected. The metropolitan countries were still the major source of investment capital, and the government funds which composed most of this capital were used to develop the 'infrastructure' of the various territories and provide basic social amenities rather than to foster any project – a growth in heavy industry, for instance – which might affect the structure of the economy. Some private investment helped to create new industries, but these were few in number and produced for the most part consumer goods. Primarily, the West African territories remained producers of basic raw materials. The Korean War and the massive rearmament programmes of the great Powers during the fifties led to a more intensive exploitation of mineral resources, so that by 1957 iron and bauxite had become a significant factor in the economy of Guinea, while sixty per cent of Sierra Leone's revenue from direct taxes in 1957–8 came from the iron-mining company there. Agricultural products were also in increased demand, however, so that their relative importance did not change very much. Moreover, within a comparatively short space of time large stocks had been accumulated and demand fell off; in 1958 the world's tin-producing countries enforced a 'quota' system and Nigerian tin production fell to half of the 1957 figure. Tables II and III below show how in the post-war period the West African economy continued to be a predominantly agrarian

Table II Imports and Exports of Selected Territories (in C.F.A. francs and £s)

Country	Year	Imports	Exports	Chief Products as % of Total Exports		% Share of Metropolitan Country in Total Trade	
						exports	imports
French West Africa(i)	1956	66,661m.	60,014m.	Groundnut products	33.8	66.0	66.0
				Coffee	26.2		
				Cocoa	14.0		
Gold Coast	1956	88.9m.	86.6m.	Cocoa	59.0	34.5	46.9
Nigeria	1957	152.5m.	127.5m.	Cocoa	20.4	61.4	43.3
				Groundnut products	19.4		
				Palm products	24.9		

(i) Individual figures not available.

one, producing raw materials for the industrial countries, in particular British and France. The trading companies remained of major importance; on the eve of independence the United Africa Company and other Unilever subsidiaries still controlled about half of Nigeria's import trade. The disparity between territories also persisted, with the Gold Coast much richer than either Nigeria or Sierra Leone, and the Ivory Coast the only French territory able to amass any financial reserves of its own.

Table III   Wage and Salary Earners as a Percentage of the Population in Selected Territories

Country	Year	African Population	No. of Wage and Salary Earners	% of Population
Senegal	1957(i)	2,181,000	52,400	2.4
Soudan	1957(i)	3,636,000	16,300	0.4
Guinea	1957(i)	2,498,000	28,700	1.1
Ivory Coast	1957(i)	2,471,000	45,000	1.8
Upper Volta	1957(i)	3,322,000	10,100	0.3
Niger	1957(i)	2,333,000	5,600	0.2
Gold Coast	1956	4,700,000	261,600(ii)	5.6(?)
Nigeria	1957	33,000,000	475,600(ii)	1.4(?)

(i) as at 1 January   (ii) returns incomplete

Breaking the Mould

We have already noted the sense of urgency felt by the new rulers of West Africa in face of the economic situation that they inherited. The call for unity and the intolerance of opposition described in previous chapters stems to a large extent from this feeling. The problem facing the new rulers is to communicate this sense of urgency to the masses, and the answer has been a call for 'mobilization', the rallying of the nation for a united effort. Here the example of party and other militants is all-important, and in the French-speaking states considerable emphasis is laid upon the formation of 'cadres' who will give a lead to the rest. Nor must it be thought that the idea of mobilization is confined to those countries which are marked by a radical leadership. In the Ivory Coast and Upper Volta new laws passed in January and February 1963 made all men and women over the age of eighteen liable to drafting into designated jobs for two years. Anyone whose conduct seemed prejudicial to the drive for development might be placed under house arrest and put to work in the public interest. Thus the most stringent measures of all have been taken not by the dedicated revolutionary but by some of those who in European terms seem most prone to *laissez faire*. In Nigeria, Sierra Leone, and Liberia the concept of mobilization is least well developed, but there are special reasons for this. In the first two states power is not yet completely monopolized and there is still party competition, so that the machinery of the State cannot be wholeheartedly devoted to the purpose. Moreover, the problems of mobilizing the enormous Nigerian population in a united effort are probably insurmountable at this stage. In Liberia President Tubman realizes the need for development, but the True Whig Party is not an appropriate instrument for general mobilization, since its objective for nearly a century has been the control of the government for the benefit of a few immigrant families, Tubman's among them.

In an atmosphere of excitement and exhortation to united effort, mobilization increasingly and inevitably acquires a military flavour, with the mood of a country at war further promoted by the use of army units for work on development projects, as in Senegal. This situation is explicitly recognized in a document from Ghana quoted above:

Independent African States are faced with urgent and pressing problems of reconstruction, for the solution of which all the available national resources both human and otherwise must be mobilized. This situation is almost analogous to a state of war and national emergency which is always met in the older established countries by the formation of coalition or national governments.[6]

Attempts are made to discover the enemy responsible for poverty and backwardness, and 'colonialism' – or, increasingly, 'neo-colonialism' – provides a convenient focus. There is a growing tendency to ascribe all set-backs and hesitations to traitors within and enemies without. Xenophobia grows, directed first of all against citizens and business enterprises of the former imperial countries; but Africans from neighbouring countries are not immune. Indeed, with the turning inward which has marked many of the new states since their attainment of independence, these neighbours are suspected of plotting to overthrow the government and thwart its efforts at development. The accusation of conspiracy with a foreign power has been a prominent one in trials of opposition leaders. Both Nigeria and Togo have accused Ghana, which in turn has accused Togo, while Guinea has levelled charges against Senegal, and Mauritania against Morocco.*

The situation that results from the campaigns for mobilization is thus often one of fluctuating tension, reaching a peak with each government campaign or the discovery of a new plot, and then abating again. Often, too, this tension appears to reflect a struggle within the governing party between the 'left' and the 'centre': the former, usually associated with the youth wing, demanding more radical measures and a speeding-up of development; the latter, made up of the more prominent leaders who control the party machine. This control usually ensures the victory of the 'centre', but the atmosphere of tension and conflict tends to exhaust the ordinary citizens, so that their response to each successive campaign seems less vigorous. During the crisis in Guinea of November 1961, criticism of Sékou Touré by elements on the 'left' in the P.D.G., on the grounds that he was not pushing forward the policy of 'socialism' and State control fast enough, coincided with demonstrations in a number of places against 'human investment'; the demonstrators claimed that work under this title hardly differed from forced labour under the French. The tours undertaken by Sékou Touré to explain his policies and redress grievances show how seriously he viewed the situation.

Nevertheless, assuming that general energies may be thus mobilized, it is one thing to achieve this mobilization and quite another to channel it in the right direction. It is here that for many of the countries of West Africa 'the Plan' becomes of such

* For the significance of this for the relations between states, see Chapter 7.

great importance. Through plans for economic development, intended to run as a series and the first timed to last for perhaps three, six, or even ten years, the new states – like most other 'under-developed' areas – hope to transform their economies. As the Nigerian National Plan put it:

> The basic objective of planning in Nigeria is not merely to accelerate the rate of economic growth and the rate at which the level of living of the population can be raised; it is also to give her an increasing measure of control over her own destiny. The present First National Plan is therefore seen as the first in a series which will bring Nigeria to the 'take-off' stage. This means that within a reasonable period of time, Nigeria should be in a position to generate, from a diversified economy, sufficient income and savings of its own to finance a steady rate of growth with no more dependence on external sources for capital or manpower than is usual to obtain through the natural incentives of international commerce.[7]

In the economic thinking of the governments of the new states this idea of 'control' looms large. In Ghana the Convention People's Party declared in 1962 that 'the basic aim of our economic development is to free our economy from alien control and domination'.[8] Whether these governments are 'radical' ones like those in Ghana and Guinea, or 'moderate', as in the Ivory Coast or Nigeria, they have tended to arrive at the same conclusions. Two processes are considered necessary. First of all, the basic control over the national economy must pass into the hands of the country's own citizens. Secondly, this economy must be transformed, reshaped so that its old mercantile character will give place to something new, and it will 'take off' into a state of growth like that described in the Nigerian Plan.

Almost all the new governments of West Africa, therefore, subscribe to the view held by the government of Mali, that 'profound reforms of structure' are necessary. They do not all agree, however, that this necessarily involves 'economic and financial decolonization, the establishment of socialist structures in the rural areas and the town, the development of a State sector in industry, transport, commerce, and finance.'[9] Admittedly, the term 'Socialist' is very widely used. It is usually regarded as something vaguely beneficial, and only in Liberia and perhaps in the Ivory Coast is it necessarily equated with a threat to the *status quo*. In some countries the term is frequently employed, but implies little more than a general desire to raise the standard of living. Thus in Nigeria the N.C.N.C. talks of 'Pragmatic Socialism' while disclaiming any intention to nationalize foreign businesses, and Chief Awolowo attempted in the first few years after independence to commit the Action Group to a 'Democratic Socialism' which included the simultaneous expropriation of foreigners and the encouragement of Nigerian private enterprise.

Nevertheless, certain states in West Africa do officially regard themselves as 'Socialist' in character. In attempting to distinguish between their economic policies and those of other states we might profitably examine their views on two related matters – the role of the State in economic development, and the nature of economic planning.

In all the West African countries it is recognized that the State must play a part in the processes of taking control of the old-style mercantile economy and transforming it into something new, capable of self-sustained growth. The classic European, American, or Japanese 'Industrial Revolutions' cannot be repeated in West Africa, because none of the new states has a group of local entrepreneurs large and experienced enough to undertake this task.[10] In the absence of such groups it is the political *élite* which must take the initiative, and it does this by using the power of the State, the machinery of which it controls. The avowedly Socialist states, of course, put the major emphasis on the activity of the State. In its first five years of independence Guinea reserved virtually all large-scale economic activity to the State. Mali moved rapidly in the same direction after 1960. Nevertheless, it must not be thought that 'State Socialism' has been confined to those countries which throughout this study have been singled out for a number of reasons as 'the radicals'. In August 1961 Mamadou Dia of Senegal declared in a speech made at Thiès that

... we are the only state which, after one year of independence, has put forward a Development Plan. In socialist construction we are in fact the most advanced African state.[11]

In Senegal the State has undertaken the buying of the ground-nut crop, replacing the middlemen with government agencies, and encouraged the formation of producer cooperatives. Unlike Guinea and Mali, however, the State has not moved directly into the field of foreign trade or the retailing of imports, and is endeavouring to encourage private investment in industry.

Private enterprise is also still envisaged as having a part to play in Ghana. The Convention People's Party has proclaimed:

The Party is firmly of the view that the planning of the national economy can only be really effective when the major means of production, distribution and exchange have been brought under the control and ownership of the State.[12]

President Nkrumah, in a speech given at Kumasi in March 1962, in fact distinguished five sectors of the economy, in only three of which the State was to be active. It was to run its own enterprises, which would provide employment, increase incomes and so standards of living, aid the State to stabilize prices and the currency, and provide such services as private enterprise could or would not provide. The State was, secondly, to establish new enterprises in partnership with foreign business interests. Thirdly, the State would be active in the cooperative sector of the economy. The remaining two sectors were to be left to private enterprise. Foreign firms which were already established would be allowed to continue their operations, though they would have to give the government the first option whenever they intended to sell all or part of their equity shares. Lastly, the sector of small-scale private enterprise would in future be reserved for Ghanaians.

Other countries would limit the role of the State even further. It is recognized that the State must inevitably play its part, but this is restricted to a few main spheres of activity: providing the essential infrastructure, mobilizing the capital for projects beyond the scope of private investment – such as the proposed Kainji Dam in Nigeria – and encouraging foreign interests to set up new enterprises, sometimes in partnership with the government. Thus the Ivory Coast has given maximum encouragement to foreign investment in industrial projects, and the industrial output in that country rose from some £10,000,000 in 1957 to about £16,000,000 in 1960. Shares in the new Abidjan oil refinery are divided among the Ivory Coast government, with a ten per cent holding; the French State Agency, B.R.P., with thirty per cent; and Shell, British Petroleum, Mobil, Texaco, and Esso, which control the remainder. As the leader of the Entente group, the Ivory Coast has been able to influence its associates in the same direction. Thus the government of Upper Volta, though it has entered the retail trade through a system of State shops, has guaranteed that there will be no nationalization of foreign enterprises. Similarly, in September 1961, the Finance Minister of Niger declared:

> Private commerce and enterprise have their assured place in Niger where the government has always recognized the essential role which they can continue to play in the country.[13]

Outside the Entente group, Mauritania relies entirely upon foreign capital, French, British, Italian, and German, grouped together in the MIFERMA combine, for the exploitation of the iron ore upon which the economic future of the country depends. Nigeria, the most populous of the West African countries, has put considerable emphasis upon the development of the private sector in its six-year National Development Plan, declaring that 'Governments are convinced that no amount of Government activity can effectively replace the efforts of a broadly based and progressive private sector.'[14]

It has already been noted that it is possible to distinguish between the new states of West Africa not only on the grounds of their attitude to the role of the State in economic development but also of their general approaches to the problem of economic planning. Thus the Senegalese Four Year Plan, adopted in May 1961, put considerable emphasis upon two particular ideas, that of *'croissance globale'* (balanced growth) and that of *'encadrement rural'* (the training of rural 'cadres' – militants who would give a lead to the rest). These two ideas, taken together with the new role of the State, were held to constitute a ' Socialist' programme. The implication of the first was that growth must be balanced in such a way as to permit an overall improvement in the standard of living. Thus a growing disparity between standards in urban and rural areas would be avoided, while it was realized that major increases in productivity would have to come, for the time being at least, from the agricultural sector of the economy. 'Rural animation' thus formed an important part of the Plan:

> Animation has for [its] general objectives to contribute to the awakening and the sensitivity of the Senegalese masses, urban and rural, to the problems of development, and to the creation of a current of the same kind among the cadres of the nation at all levels.[15]

The Mali government has entertained much the same view of planning. Indeed, although Mali's Five Year Plan was conceived after the break-up of the Mali Federation between Senegal and Soudan, and although Senegal's plan was produced by a team under the leadership of a French Catholic priest and Mali's by a French Marxist economist, the plans of the two states are remarkably similar. The Malian Plan, adopted in August 1961, is also based on an effort to increase rural productivity, upon the formation of cooperatives, and *encadrement rural*. As a report on the Plan put it:

> The setting-up of this new cooperative organization will require action for the training of cadres and for education led by the public powers and the full range of political organization (Party, Trade Unions, Youth and Women's Organizations, etc.).[16]

An important difference between Senegal and Mali, however, is that the dominant party in Mali, the Union Soudanaise–R.D.A., has been militant and well-organized enough to provide an effective instrument for mobilizing the country from the bottom upwards. This has not been true of Senegal's U.P.S., and this factor must have contributed considerably to the 'disequilibriums, distortions, and delays' in the Plan, announced by President Senghor in April 1963.

The implied view of the Nigerian Plan on the formation of 'cadres' gives a clue to the nature of a second main approach to economic planning. In its introductory discussion on 'The Need for Planning', the Plan states:

> Governments may govern, economists may plan, administrators may organize, but ultimately the execution of all plans, no matter how well designed and intentioned, depends upon the response of the people themselves. The Plan can give a sense of purpose, direction

and urgency; it must establish priorities and overall magnitudes; it must coordinate the activity of Government in relation to the overall objectives. But its ultimate success will depend not so much upon these factors as upon the involvement of the people and the willingness of men and women in all walks of life, in Government and in private business, to dedicate themselves to the common purpose.[17]

This view places relatively less stress upon the activity of the State in forming cadres at all levels, and relatively more on voluntary enterprise. The Nigerian Plan puts its trust more in the indirect techniques of fiscal control than in the direct mobilization of human resources; the federal Finance Minister's 'Mobilization Budget' of 1962 was intended to mobilize capital, not people. Nor do we find an emphasis upon 'balanced growth', but rather upon the importance of certain key projects, on which the future expansion of the economy will depend. Thus the Kainji Dam and hydro-electric project has been described as the 'cornerstone' of the Federal part of the Plan, and is the most expensive single item (£68.1 million). In the same way the Volta River project occupies a central place in any Ghanaian development plan.

The presence of Senegal in one category and Ghana in another prevents an equating of 'socialist' views on the role of the State directly with the concepts of overall growth and the training of cadres, or 'project planning' with limitations upon the State's activities. Rather, it may tentatively be suggested that what is to be seen here is a difference between 'French' and 'British' planning, between a centralizing approach based upon a theoretical, almost a philosophical attitude to development problems, and a pragmatic approach which believes in dispersing initiative. Ghana, of course, has modified this second approach, particularly in the last respect, through the Marxist intellectual influence upon Kwame Nkrumah and other leaders, and through the use of Polish and Hungarian advisers.

Whether it adopts a formal Plan or not, the new West African state still faces its two problems – the assertion of control over the old mercantile economy and its ultimate transformation. In order to achieve this, many measures may be adopted, either as part of a Plan or independently. Most West African states have adopted some of these; a few of them, a very wide range. There is a common tendency, for example, to try and diversify patterns of trade and to seek new sources of technical assistance and capital investment. This is, of course, a response to one of the basic features of the old 'colonial' economy, the way in which the former possession remains linked with the metropolitan country. The most dramatic shift of emphasis in trade during the first few years after independence has been that of Guinea.

Table IV   Guinea: Trade with France, 1958–61 (as % of total trade)

	1958	1959	1960	1961
Exports	69.0	57.0	28.2	17.8
Imports	78.0	62.5	29.9	12.2

Considering the nature of Guinea's political break with France, it is not difficult to understand the change shown here. Ghana has also made efforts to diversify its trade, and a comparison between its exports of cocoa and those of Nigeria is instructive. In the year ending 30 September 1961, four main purchasers (the United Kingdom, the U.S.A., Western Germany, and the Netherlands) accounted for 91.0 per cent of Nigeria's cocoa exports. Ghana, more dependent upon this one crop than Nigeria, had obviously sought to spread its exports more widely, and sold relatively less to the United Kingdom (11.7 per cent compared with Nigeria's 23.3 per cent) and the Netherlands (13.1 per cent compared with 18.1 per cent). Small amounts were sold to a large number of countries: of those worth listing individually, eleven countries each bought amounts constituting less than two per cent of the total; Nigeria sold comparable quantities to only two countries. Nigeria sold appreciable amounts only to Italy (including shippings through Trieste), France, and Canada in addition to the four countries mentioned above. Ghana sold to fifteen others, including the U.S.S.R. (two per cent of the total), Poland, Japan, and Israel.

As with trade, so with investment and technical aid; the states of West Africa are seeking these essentials in a variety of places, with the 'radicals' – Ghana, Guinea, and Mali – showing themselves the most ready to seek aid from the Communist bloc. In September 1960, for instance, Guinea secured a loan of about £9,000,000 from the People's Republic of China. In March 1961 an agreement between Mali and the U.S.S.R. gave Mali forty million roubles worth of credits (approximately £16 million), and the promise of aid for various industrial projects in the Mali Plan. In September of the same year an agreement between Ghana and the U.S.S.R. pledged Soviet help in setting up state farms, increasing rice, maize, and cotton production, and building a tractor and a ferro-manganese works.

Nevertheless, diversification of trade, investment, and technical aid has not only – or even primarily – involved the Communist bloc. Links are increasingly being sought with the U.S.A., West Germany, Israel, and others which are either completely free from an imperial past or else have had enough time to live it down. The European Economic Community is also becoming of increasing significance through its own Development Fund, and to some extent is beginning to replace France as a source of capital for the French-speaking states associated with it. As will be seen in Chapter 7, however, the extent to which these, and the other West African states, will ultimately be able to reduce their dependence on the old metropolitan countries remains a matter for conjecture.

The new states not only seek to change their patterns of trade; they are also attempting to change the nature of their exports and imports. At present they have no alternative but to recognize that for the immediate future they will have to remain primarily exporters of raw materials, not of finished goods. This means that the best that can be done is to increase production, and to try and find new materials for export. The future significance of iron ore exports for the economies of Liberia, Sierra Leone, and Mauritania, for instance, or of oil for Nigeria, is likely to be great. At the same time the new states have begun to try and eliminate competition among themselves. Thus in January 1962 Ghana, Nigeria, the Ivory Coast, Cameroun, and Brazil formed a Cocoa Producers' Alliance, while in June Senegal and Nigeria agreed to set up an African Groundnut Council.

Most attention has been paid to the problem of imports. With the exception of the Ivory Coast, the countries of West Africa have tended to show an adverse balance of trade in recent years. This is not surprising since nearly all of them have launched ambitious programmes of economic development, necessitating increased imports of foreign products like machinery and fuel oil. Foreign exchange reserves, however, are small, and increased imports mean a balance of payments problem. Many imports are non-essential goods, while some of the French-speaking states – Guinea and Senegal, for instance – have to import large quantities of basic foodstuffs. The control of imports has thus become necessary, and various measures have been adopted. The most obvious response, of course, has been a policy of selective tariffs, with heavy import duties on luxury goods and other non-essentials. Guinea for some time actually took the whole import trade (as well as exports) out of the hands of the foreign companies, and replaced them with State corporations. These were originally two in number, the Guinean External and Internal Trade Agencies, but in March 1961 they were abolished, after President Touré admitted that their inability to handle goods had meant a piling-up of over 100,000 tons on the Conakry wharves. In June 1961 four new State companies were established to handle the importation of goods like textiles and building materials, and a number of others were subsequently also created. An alternative method, adopted in Mali, has been to give State companies a monopoly over sugar, cement, salt, matches, cigarettes, and other commodities. Ghana has not set up companies of this kind, although like the other countries (and Upper Volta), it has established a system of State shops. The Ghanaian government has relied instead upon close control over import licensing, and in December 1961 it replaced the old Open General and Quota Licences with a system under which individual items are licensed.

These measures represent a degree of State activity in the import trade which many of the new governments are not prepared to accept. Most of them, as far as their resources permit, have attempted to reduce imports by establishing factories and mills – usually in partnership with foreign concerns – which can manufacture or assemble consumer goods on the spot. Beer, tiles, cement, cheap textiles, tinned meat and fish, as well as many other commodities are now produced in a number of West African states, while Ghana, Nigeria, and the Ivory Coast also boast their own car and lorry assembly plants.

Government participation in new ventures, however, represents a relatively small part of economic activity. The foreign companies, as we have seen, were still dominant at the time of independence, and the assertion of control by the government must ultimately mean the extension of control over them. For some years, indeed, Guinea had a policy of direct nationalization, and there diamond and iron mining, transport, and electricity and water supplies were then all brought under public control. In Mali and Senegal foreign traders have been pushed out of groundnut buying by new State agencies. In Ghana a new Mines (Amendment) Act made acquisition by the State possible after certain goldmines had been threatened with closure by expatriate companies early in 1961.

A number of countries have also been concerned to control the repatriation of profits by foreign firms. In March 1962 the Ghana government laid down that at least sixty per cent of gross profits had to be reinvested in Ghana every year, in addition to company tax and compulsory savings. Even the Ivory Coast, usually most liberal in its dealings with foreign business concerns, found it necessary to announce an extra levy on their profits in January 1962, since there had been a movement of capital during 1961 of 10,000,000,000 C.F.A. francs into the country and 19,000,000,000 out of it.

In addition to controlling the repatriation of profits, most states have sought to secure a more firm control over their monetary policies. Thus Ghana, Nigeria, and Sierra Leone successively withdrew from the old West African Currency Board after independence, but have found it advantageous to retain their membership of the sterling area. Most of the French-speaking countries entered into an agreement on a common currency, the C.F.A. ('African Financial Community') franc, in May 1962, and have remained within the franc zone. Guinea had already established its own currency and left the franc zone on 1 March 1960, however, and on 1 July 1962, Mali also adopted its own franc, though remaining within the franc zone. The creation of new financial institutions, such as the Nigerian Central Bank, the Société Dahoméenne de Banque or the Banque de Développement Nigérienne, has greatly increased State control of financial matters. In 1962 the Nigerian Central Bank was given new powers to control the liquidity ratios of the commercial banks (the most important of them expatriate-owned) and so indirect control over their provision of credit facilities. Despite these new controls some states have experienced considerable balance of payments problems. Ghana, Guinea, and Mali have all imposed stringent regulations upon the import and export of currency, and in April 1963 the government of Guinea was forced to revalue its currency. In the following month a series of agreements signed by France and Guinea greatly strengthened the foreign exchange position of the latter by granting it a credit of 1,500,000,000 C.F.A. francs.

Measures taken by the West African states to gain further control over their own economies include, of course, the development not only of State banks but of a whole range of new institutions. As one survey of the position in Mali put it:

... the present structures inherited from tradition and colonization are ossified and represent the essential obstacle to every serious effort to increase production.[18]

Structures have to be changed and new institutions created, particularly as the State plays an ever larger part in economic development. Some of these institutions have already been mentioned – State trading corporations, State factories, State farms – but in addition there is an endless proliferation of development banks, cooperatives of one sort or another, and agencies for buying and marketing. All of these are being added to already existing institutions, and here the English-speaking countries may enjoy some advantage, since they have the foundations of the colonially created system of public boards and corporations upon which to build. Nevertheless, as was shown in the last chapter, the institutional pattern throughout West Africa is still confused, particularly in relation to the role of the dominant party. The demands of economic development are not only demands for skilled men and huge supplies of capital, enormously important though these may be. They are also demands for a stable, smooth-running political and administrative system which can support the complex process of development and the effort it demands. One of the most vital questions for the future will be whether or not the ruling *élite* is able – and unselfish – enough to meet this challenge and evolve systems of government adequate for the task.

6 Education and Manpower

Economic development in West Africa must not be regarded solely in terms of the diversification of trade patterns, the more efficient exploitation of land and mineral resources, and the establishment of industries. It has already been indicated that the human factor also is of vital importance in the phenomenon of mobilization. As the draft version of the Ghanaian *First Seven-Year Development Plan* put it:

... we must look to industry and agriculture, to provide an increased standard of living, but these two sectors of the economy are dependent on an adequate supply of suitably educated and trained manpower. In a sense education takes precedence over the other two as the mainspring of economic progress.[1]

Or as an acute observer has said:

The most difficult problem for the development of the 'hidden productive forces' of the Black Continent lies in its human potentialities and qualities.[2]

Whatever there is to be done people must do it, and under modern conditions such people must often be trained. Projects must be planned, surveyors must prepare the site, engineers must direct the project, foremen must take charge of labour gangs. High-grade and middle-grade manpower is essential to economic development. Administrators, engineers, doctors, agricultural experts, accountants, surveyors, university and secondary school teachers on the one hand, laboratory technicians, primary school teachers, agricultural assistants, clerks, draftsmen, and foremen on the other, all of these are needed, and all of them have to be given a modern education, often a specialized one. Throughout Africa such people are urgently needed, for at present there are far too few of them. An immediate task facing the new states, therefore, is to model – or rather to remodel – their educational systems to meet the ever growing demands for skilled manpower.

Another problem exists – not of quality, like the one mentioned above, but a problem of quantity. On the one hand there is the problem of finding enough skilled men and women to fill the vacancies, and on the other that of finding enough jobs to absorb the large numbers of unemployed and under-employed people existing in West African society. The manpower planner sees two basic distortions in the West African economies. First, there are not enough trained people to provide the indispensable framework upon which all development must rest. Secondly, development is not rapid enough to provide work for all those who need it. It is obvious that these two factors are very closely connected.

The Colonial Heritage

As with so much else, the new states of West Africa inherited their systems of modern education from the withdrawing colonial Powers. This in itself has been of great significance, as will be shown later, but there is another inheritance which must first be considered, since it underlies the educational system itself, and that is the nature of manpower in the colonial economy.

Certain features of the population structure taken as a whole are, of course, related only indirectly to the impact of colonial rule. Thus the growth in population may be related to basic improvements in health and sanitation which have reduced the death rate. The population of the West African countries is growing rapidly; estimates for a number of countries (Ghana, Nigeria, Senegal) put the rate of growth at two to three per cent annually. Every year sees the need to give education to more and more children and find employment for more and more school-leavers. This in itself constitutes a major problem. The population of West Africa is also young; in Ghana one out of every two people is aged twenty or below, and one in four is aged four or less. This means that the proportion of the population which is actually at work is small, and this proportion has to carry the burden of supporting not only the relatively few who are too old to work, but the many who are too young.

More directly a result of the colonial system than the structure of the population was the use to which manpower was put in the colonial economy. The West African territories developed primarily as suppliers of raw materials and markets for manufactured goods. Most people, therefore, continued to work on the land, as they had always done, and European enterprise was seldom involved directly in agricultural production. The cocoa, cotton, groundnuts, and palm oil were produced by peasant farmers, working on a small scale. This contrasts strongly with other African territories, such as Kenya, where about eighty per cent of the cash crops were produced on European farms. Although many West Africans took the opportunity presented by the increased economic activity of the colonial period to become petty traders, or craftsmen, or wage-earners of one sort or another, most people remained directly dependent upon the land for a living. It was estimated in 1963 that about sixty per cent of the working population of Ghana fell into this last category, and Ghana was not, in fact, typical in this respect. Even Senegal, with an estimated three quarters of its working population engaged in farming and stock-rearing in 1961, had far more people working in non-agricultural jobs than most of the other French-speaking countries.

African economic activity, therefore, as it developed during the colonial period, was typically agricultural and small in scale, and this small scale was generally true even of non-agricultural activities. As the Ghanaian draft Seven Year Development Plan put it:

Ghana's food is produced by small-scale peasant farmers; the processing of this food is done in small-scale family establishments; household goods, when locally made, are produced in small street-corner factories.[3]

In this situation the demand for skilled labour was relatively small. Such skills as were needed for petty trading could be acquired mainly by experience, and craftsmen were usually trained as apprentices to established men. In British West Africa, particularly in the southern Gold Coast and Western Nigeria, an impressive development of the cooperative movement among farmers gave an opportunity to develop organizational skills and to spread knowledge of new techniques, particularly in pest-control. In French West Africa, however, some observers consider that the cooperative movement was hampered because of the lack of farmers with even a minimal education, and because in some areas the traditional authorities – the *marabouts* of the Mūridiyya order in Senegal, for example – took control of the cooperatives.[4] Although both the British and French administrations made considerable efforts to improve the efficiency of farmers, particularly in the last years before independence, productivity had generally been high enough to meet the demand for cash crops, if not for food in some territories, without such efforts.

The educational systems which developed alongside this economic structure during most of the colonial period were more or less adequate to meet the demands upon them. They were not adequate, however, to meet the need for increased agricultural productivity, the development of industries, and the promotion of basic social welfare programmes which arose after 1945 and especially after independence. In order to appreciate this, the colonial systems of education, as they developed up to 1939, may be examined from three different points of view – the intentions behind them, the content of their teaching, and the extent to which facilities were available.

The intentions of the colonial schools were quite simple. As was seen in Chapter 2, they were established in order to produce the type of manpower needed by a colonial economy and administration. This was true whether the schools were established by missions or by the governments themselves. The need was a limited one. Africans could not usually expect to reach the highest levels of employment in the administration or business, and the demand was mainly for clerks and primary school teachers. As one prominent Nigerian politician has written:

In my part of the world at that time, the élite of society were the pastors, catechists, teachers, clerks and interpreters. They were respected, admired and adored. The *summum bonum* of a Christian parent's ambition was that his son should, after leaving school, be like one of them.[5]

Almost all the important policy-making and managerial positions were in the hands of Europeans. Even the more advanced levels of education were mainly staffed by European teachers. (Thus in 1954 the staff of secondary schools in French West Africa was made up of twenty Africans and 130 expatriates.) Moreover, the number of people employed at these higher levels of responsibility was relatively small. Professor Harbison has estimated that in Nigeria shortly after independence some 30,000 people, one third of them still expatriates, were carrying the entire burden of top-level policy decisions and administrative responsibility. This is less than 0.1 per cent of the population: in Ghana the comparable figure was 0.3 per cent; in India, 0.5 per cent; in the developed countries, between two and five per cent. The Ghana draft Plan made the same point when it declared:

> The profile of employment in 1960 shows a particularly small proportion of employment in managerial, technical, craftsman and supervisory grades. These are precisely the elements in the total labour force on whom the economy depends most for its productive efficiency and its ability to grow.[6]

The system of education in operation throughout most of the colonial period, therefore, tended to produce Africans trained only to take subordinate positions. Institutions like the École William Ponty in Senegal or the Yaba Higher College in Nigeria could produce enough advanced students to fill any higher positions open to Africans, like the twenty secondary school teaching posts mentioned above. Even though the last decade of colonial rule saw an attempt to provide more advanced education – the opening of University Colleges in Nigeria and the Gold Coast, and the Institute of Higher Studies at Dakar – at independence there were not enough trained people to staff a modern administrative structure and at the same time pursue any ambitious plans for economic development.

Moreover, many of those who had received an advanced education had been given an unsuitable training for the tasks which lay ahead. Since one of the few careers open without restriction to the able African had been law, many had sought a legal training. Thus in 1963 there were over 1,000 indigenous lawyers in Nigeria, about a third of them concentrated in Lagos alone. Of even greater significance, perhaps, nearly 900 Nigerians were currently studying law. To become a barrister was associated in the young man's mind with success. Accustomed to see expatriates hold all senior technical posts, he was much less likely to think of becoming an engineer or agricultural expert.

Not only the intentions of colonial education but its content had predisposed Africans to think this way. Designed mainly to produce clerks, it was literary rather than practical or vocational. It may have provided Africans, as Guy Hunter has argued, with 'the entry to the heritage of political and religious experience of mankind'.[7] It also, however, gave rise to two attitudes towards education which boded ill for the needs of the new states after independence. First of all, people tended to believe that the only genuine education was a literary one, and that any form of education which included some measure of practical training was inferior. Secondly, manual labour was often felt to be undignified for the educated man. A school diploma was the passport to the town and the life of the white-collar worker, an escape from the drudgery of the farm. Such attitudes may be understandable in a colonial situation, but they constitute a serious problem for the newly independent states. As a Senegalese publication has put it:

At the moment that our country became independent, it was necessary to launch an appeal to all educators, and more particularly to the masters of our primary schools ... to teach our youth the value of effort and to show them that what must be honoured even more than the diploma is work. The road of national construction and true independence passes through the training of cadres, without which the life of the country cannot be assured nor its independence guaranteed.[8]

One final feature of West African education in the colonial period must be noted – its extent. As was pointed out in Chapter 2, to get any education at all in the colonial period was a privilege. Table V shows the percentage of school-age children at school in selected territories during the later years of the colonial

period.* It can be seen that on the whole there were more widely
spread facilities for some sort of education in British West Africa
than in the French territories. Nevertheless, even within the
British territories distribution might be very uneven; in Sierra
Leone some fifty-five per cent of the school-age children were at
school in the Colony area during 1948, while the figure for the
Protectorate was only four per cent. All over West Africa most
people in all but the most privileged areas were illiterate when
colonial rule entered its last decade. Despite increased attempts
to open schools and start programmes of adult education in these
last ten years, the great majority was still illiterate when independence was attained.

Table V   School attendance in Selected Territories

French West Africa, 1947		British West Africa, 1950	
Territory	Per cent	Territory	Per cent
Senegal	12.4	Nigeria	21.4
Soudan	5.0	Gold Coast	43.6
Mauritania	2.7		
Ivory Coast	3.7		
Dahomey	10.0		

The Nationalist Reaction

It was natural, indeed inevitable, that the nationalist parties
should react to the inherited problems of education and manpower in two main ways – by a desire to replace expatriates in
senior positions of control with Africans and a desire to spread
the benefits of a modern education much more widely than
before.

Africanization of posts has in fact proceeded more rapidly in
English-speaking than in French-speaking West Africa. Table
VI shows the situation after Ghana had been independent for

* It has been assumed here, following official practice, that children of school-age
represent some fifteen per cent of the population. In fact recent research in Nigeria
seems to suggest that the correct proportion might be at least twice this figure. In
the general absence of reliable censuses, any calculation based on population statistics
must be treated with caution.

five years, Nigeria for eighteen months, and Sierra Leone for slightly more than a year. Two points should be remembered.

Table VI   Pensionable Expatriate Officers in Former British Territories

	At Independence	In mid 1962
Ghana	580	30
Nigeria: Federation	870	555
North	900	640
East	105	90
West	135	110
Sierra Leone	250	115
Totals	2,840	1,540

First, the process had already begun in the last few years of colonial rule, but had progressed much farther in some areas than in others. This explains, for instance, the low numbers of expatriates in the two southern Regions of Nigeria as compared with the North. Secondly, although the number of expatriates holding pensionable positions may have declined after independence, the number of these on specific contracts has often increased. The English-speaking states cannot in fact hope to undertake extensive development programmes without the aid of expatriate technicians. Though nationalist pride may to some extent be assuaged by the employment of Americans, Russians, Israelis, and others not associated with the colonial past, indigenous experts are in no way numerous enough to permit of complete Africanization.

In most of the French-speaking states this has been recognized more readily. Only in Guinea and Mali have Frenchmen been almost entirely replaced, with the administrative structure Africanized and most of the technical experts employed since independence being Russians, Chinese, and others from the Communist countries. Replacement of French officials has naturally caused some strain, since the supply of trained Africans has been so small. In Mali the need to draft Administrative Secretaries from the Ministries in Bamako to act as circle commandants, and some of the Administrative, Financial, and

Accountancy Clerks as *arrondissement* chiefs meant that at the end of 1961 the numbers of the former were twenty per cent short of what was required, and of the latter thirty per cent, without considering further expansion. In Senegal the same problem of vacancies in the civil service, leading to a rush of teachers to fill them, resulted in a decision in November 1960 to pay a twenty per cent bonus to teachers remaining in the classroom.

In most of these states, however, Frenchmen have remained as 'technical councillors', and even in Mali are still prominent in education. Table VII shows the composition of school personnel in Mali during the school year 1960–1. The vital importance of French teachers in secondary education shows very

Table VII   School personnel in Mali, 1960–1

	Malians	French	Others	Total
State Primary Schools	1,247	34	7	1,288
Private Primary Schools	109	51	8	168
State Secondary Schools	45	79	5	129
Private Secondary Schools	16	35	13	64
Total	1,417	199	33	1,649

Note: Adapted from *The Educated African* (q.v.), Table 1, page 496

plainly. Although in Mali the numbers of Frenchmen may have declined somewhat since 1961, the provision of teachers – paid for by the French taxpayer – is still an important service rendered by France to her former possessions. At the beginning of 1962, for example, it was estimated that the cost to France of teachers in Africa and Madagascar was some £14 million a year.

Nationalist enthusiasm for Africanization has had to be tempered by a recognition of the lack of suitably trained replacements. Similarly, the drive to extend educational facilities has encountered serious difficulties. Widespread illiteracy is regarded as a shameful relic of the colonial period, and vigorous steps have been taken to deal with the problem, partly through adult education, to remedy an existing evil, and partly through the building of new schools, to prevent its perpetuation. Again, these steps were initiated even before independence was actually attained. Although they already have a higher proportion of their children in school than the French-speaking states, Nigeria and Ghana have made particularly great efforts in this respect. Table VIII shows the proportions of capital expenditure under their current programmes allocated by various countries to three important spheres of social and economic development. Similarly, while the Ivory Coast was devoting 10.0 per cent of its

Table VIII   Capital Expenditure in Current Development Programmes

	Education	Primary Production	Trade and Industry
Nigeria	10.3%	13.6%	13.4%
Ghana	13.2%	14.0%	22.9%
Senegal	6.7%	13.4%	44.4%
Guinea	7.3%	22.1%	21.2%

annual budget to education in 1960, Niger 9.8 per cent, Senegal 16.0 per cent and Upper Volta 23.0 per cent, the Eastern and Western Regions of Nigeria were devoting over forty per cent of theirs, and the Northern Region over twenty-five per cent (education in Nigeria being primarily a regional matter). Sierra Leone was closer to the French-speaking states, devoting sixteen per cent of its budget to education.

Table IX   School Attendance in Selected Countries at Independence (as per cent)

French-speaking(i)		English-Speaking	
Senegal	28.5	Nigeria(ii)	55.6
Mali	10.0	Sierra Leone(iii)	25.3
Mauritania	8.3		
Ivory Coast	43.0		
Dahomey	35.9		
Niger	6.7		

(i) Figures for 1960   (ii) 1959–60   (iii) 1960–1

Nor have these efforts been without results. Table IX gives the number of children of school-age actually at school during the transition from colonial rule to independence. (This may be compared with Table (V) on page 136.) A better – since more accurate – indication can be derived from a study of the growth of education in Ghana during a decade which represents the last six years of colonial rule and the first four years of independence. Table X shows this, at the various levels of the educational system.

Table X   Growth of Education in Ghana, 1951–61

	1951	1961	% increase
Primary Pupils	154,360	481,500	211.9
Middle Pupils	66,175	160,000	141.7
Secondary and Technical Pupils	3,559	19,143	437.8
Teacher Training Colleges	1,916	4,552	137.5
Universities	208	1,204	478.8
Total	226,218	666,399	

Note: Adapted from the draft First Seven-Year Development Plan, Chapter 2, page 2, Table 2.1

Throughout West Africa, then, it can be seen that as the African leaders gained more and more political power in their territories, culminating in the assumption of complete control with independence, they sought to expand educational facilities. This had, of course, been one of their promises as nationalist leaders, and to a greater or lesser extent they sought to keep their promises. Yet such a policy has not been without its adverse effects. In particular it has put a very considerable strain upon the limited financial resources available. Nigeria provides a good example here. In the Western Region the Action Group government started a scheme of universal, free, compulsory primary education as early as January 1955. The most recent census figures, dating from 1952, suggested a potential enrolment of 170,000. In fact 392,000 children were enrolled in primary schools for

1955. Expenditure on education rose from £2,223,000 in 1953–4 to £5,359,000 in 1954–5, and the compulsory aspect of primary education went by the board. The Eastern Region suffered a similar experience, when the government tried to introduce free and universal primary education in 1957. In the first year the cost was fourteen per cent higher than the estimate, fees were reintroduced for Standards I–VI in 1958, and riots followed. Even then, 42.7 per cent of the total budget for 1959–60 had to be devoted to education. In French-speaking West Africa, Upper Volta was spending 23.0 per cent of its budget in 1960 in order to educate a quarter of the school-age children, and Soudan/Mali 18.0 per cent in order to educate a tenth.

The Demands of Modernity

The demands for Africanization of posts and increased educational opportunities represent one type of pressure upon the new rulers of West Africa. There is another set of pressures, of which they are also aware, although this awareness has tended to grow with independence itself, rather than during the period of the nationalist movement. Full responsibility for the direction of affairs brings with it the realization that if the new states are ever to attain modern standards of efficiency and social welfare, then certain measures must be taken to increase the supply of trained manpower.

First of all we may note the simple demand of sheer humanity. Life in West Africa – as in the other under-developed areas – is poor, nasty, brutish, and short for most people. Modern sanitation, water and electricity supplies, medical services, more and better food, all of these are crying needs. Yet none of these needs can be met without trained manpower. To take the example of medicine, at the end of 1961 there were 1,128 registered doctors and dental surgeons in Nigeria, and some 500 in Ghana. Of the 1,079 Nigerian doctors it was estimated that just over 700 were practising, though ten per cent of these were in purely administrative jobs. Over half of them were expatriates. The ratio of doctors to potential patients was thus one to 48,000: this is misleading, however, since the ratio in Lagos was one to 2,000; in the West, one to 25,000; in the East, one to 46,000; and in the North, one to 140,000. These figures may be compared with figures of one doctor to every 1,100 people in the United Kingdom, one to every 800 in the U.S.A., one to 1,250 in Sweden, and one to 2,500 in Egypt. In 1962 Nigeria was producing about fifty qualified doctors annually, and the National Development Plan adopted in that year set aside £4,870,000 for the expansion of teaching facilities so as to produce two hundred every year.

In the long run the best way to improve the standard of living is by the more effective exploitation of resources, human as well as material, and as was suggested at the beginning of this chapter, this is possible only when the necessary high-and middle-grade manpower is available. The more ambitious the Plan, the more of these are needed, though every country in West Africa is short of trained men and women of all kinds. Ghana, where even in the colonial period a larger proportion of children was at school than anywhere else in West Africa, starts therefore with an initial advantage here. Table XI shows the output of various levels of manpower in the decade 1951–61. Though these figures are impressive enough, Ghana's needs will be far greater. The future economic development envisaged in the first Seven-Year Plan is extremely ambitious, entailing the transformation of Ghana at the end of a series of such plans into an industrialized country making its living by the export of manufactured goods. To lay the manpower foundations for this would require, it was estimated, the production of about 35,000 trained teachers in the Plan period, about 1,200 senior technicians, and at least 10,000 university graduates.

In other countries the demands are more modest, but the problems no less great. In Mali, for instance, the public service had more than fifty vacancies at the end of 1961 to be filled by holders of the *baccalauréat* (the highest qualification obtainable at a secondary school). In 1960 twenty-two Malian students had taken this examination, and eighteen had passed. Nor was the shortage of trained manpower confined to the public sector. Between November 1960 and May 1961 twenty-six trained men left private employment for the public sector, and between 1959 and 1961 seven of the twelve given special training by the Bamako Chamber of Commerce changed to government service.

Table XI   Manpower Output in Ghana, 1951–61

	1951	1961	% increase
With Middle School certificate	6,400	26,500	314.0
With Technical School certificate	719	858	19.3
With Secondary School certificate	413	3,430	730.8
With University degrees	6	148	2,366.7

Note: Adapted from the draft First Seven-Year Development Plan, Chapter 2, p. 2, Table 2.1

An ultimate result of the drive to modernize the countries of West Africa will be a basic change in the composition of the labour force, entailing a reduction in the high proportion of working people employed in agriculture, and a corresponding increase in wage-earning manpower, especially skilled workers. In the more advanced of these countries the demand for skilled manpower already indicates the direction in which the economy is travelling. In Nigeria a sample Employment Market Survey carried out in March 1961 reported more than 16,000 vacancies, in only 6,000 of which were special qualifications or training not required. There were vacancies, for example, for 1,550 science and engineering technicians and 585 architects, engineers, and surveyors. In 1963 Ghana began seriously to tackle the problem of changing the country's manpower structure. The government announced its intention to increase the numbers of the essential trained personnel, particularly in the fields of transport, communications, and the semi-skilled crafts. The number of unskilled workers was to be kept constant by young men leaving the land, while the decline in the number employed in agriculture would be met by mechanization and improved farming methods.

No other country in West Africa could afford to be as ambitious as Ghana. For most of them – except possibly Nigeria – the immediate problem was to find enough trained men and women to take the first steps in the desired development and expansion of the old-style mercantile economy. Nevertheless, if all goes well, and if that economy is in fact gradually transformed, it will become necessary for them, some time perhaps in the next decade, to plan the complete re-structuring of the labour force. Even in Ghana the new 1963 Plan claimed only that it would 'make a start on the task of bringing the supply of jobs more into line with the demand for jobs'.[9] It has already been realized in Ghana, Nigeria, Senegal, and some other West African states that manpower planning is essential. This is the final demand of modernity that may be noted, the demand that urgent attention be paid to this problem. Manpower planning is impossible without adequate data, and one of the first tasks must be to collect these. Accurate censuses are essential, and it is this which made the fiasco of the 1962 Nigerian census so unfortunate. The Nigerian government in September 1960 had decided to establish a National Manpower Board, made up of representatives of the Regional Ministries of Education and Economic Development, the Federal Ministry of Labour, the universities, industry, and labour. By the end of 1962 the Board was in operation, but without a reasonably accurate idea of the country's population structure, it had to work in a vacuum.

Responses to the Problem

As the pressures for change made themselves felt in the first years of independence, the governments of the new states began to respond. In fact, however, two sets of demands were being made, the demands of modernity and the demands of nationalism. Attempts to reform the educational system, for example, were governed by demands for improvements in both quality and quantity, and the policy of the new rulers in these early years may be seen as an attempt to combine – though not necessarily to balance – the two.

Thus, in the case of university education it was fully realized by all countries that more graduates were urgently needed. This could be achieved in two ways – by expanding facilities in West Africa itself, and by sending more students abroad. As has already been noted, Ghana made plans to have at least 10,000 graduates by 1970. In Nigeria the Ashby Commission on Post-School Certificate and Higher Education proposed in 1960 that there should be 7,500 students in Nigerian universities by 1970, and the government increased this target figure to 10,000. The University College of Ibadan increased its student numbers from 1,250 in 1960–1 to 1,644 in 1961–2, and the new university at Nsukka from 225 to 896. Furthermore, the advice of the Ashby Commission that two more universities be opened, one in Lagos and one in the North, was accepted by the Federal government, with the addition, however, of another in the West. Ghana reorganized its higher education in 1961 to add the Kwame Nkrumah University of Science and Technology and the University College of Cape Coast to the already-existing University of Ghana. The University of Dakar had 1,285 students in 1959–60 and 1,398 in 1960–1, but these numbers are deceptive, since in the latter year almost a third (thirty-one per cent) of its students were French, sons and daughters of the comparatively large group of French residents in Senegal. In addition to Dakar, by the end of 1963 two new universities had been opened in French-speaking West Africa, at Abidjan in the Ivory Coast and Yaoundé in Cameroun.

The number of students abroad is difficult to estimate, since this includes not only those holding scholarships, of whom some record is kept, but also many young men and women who travel abroad on private means. Senegal had 220 students at French universities in 1961, eighty of them working for science degrees. In 1961–2 there were 523 Ghanaian students enrolled in the United Kingdom, about 240 in the U.S.A. and Canada, 300 in West and East Germany, 200 in the U.S.S.R., and about twenty in Yugoslavia. It was estimated at the beginning of 1962 that there were some 8,000 African students in France, the majority of them from West Africa, though this included those taking courses in institutions other than universities. Some 8,000 students from Nigeria alone were in the United Kingdom in mid-1963.

Although the number of West African university students is increasing, the manpower planner must be concerned at the

distribution of their subjects. Africa's primary need is for doctors, engineers, scientists, and agricultural experts, not for
lawyers and literary critics. Table XII shows the distribution
among faculties in various universities during the academic year
1960–1, the period in which most countries became independent.
The preponderance of students in the faculties of Arts and (at

Table XII   Distribution between University Faculties, 1960–1
(as %)

	Law	Medi-cine	Arts	Science	Agri-culture	Econ-omics
University College, Ibadan	—	18.9	28.8	22.2	6.6	8.2
University College of Sierra Leone	—	—	38.4	27.8	—	28.8
University of Dakar	42.1	11.0	23.0	23.9	—	(i)

(i) Taught only in an attached Institute of Applied Economic and
Commercial Sciences

Dakar) Law might not be a cause for comment in more developed
economies. In West Africa, however, the fact that subjects like
Agriculture or Medicine are either not taught at all or have comparatively few students constitutes a considerable danger. The
government of Guinea at least seems to have realized this. Having
made the decision not to found a university in its own country,
but to rely on sending students abroad, it has taken care to direct
them into studies which are regarded as important for the country's future development. Thus 560 of the 794 Guinean students
abroad in 1960 were receiving technical training, most of which,
however, would not be at university level. The remaining 234
were mainly working for a degree, and of these seventy-two were
in education, forty-eight in medicine and pharmacy, thirty-
three in the natural sciences, forty-seven in economics and
politics, and only thirty-four in the liberal arts.

There is another level, that of secondary and technical
education, which should produce the necessary middle-grade

manpower. As in the case of Guinea, some of this education may be obtained abroad, and in 1961 Senegal had 168 students in France taking courses in such subjects as printing, public health, and journalism. Middle-grade manpower is required in much greater numbers than this, however, and ultimately it is far less expensive to provide most of the training at home than to send students abroad. Thus the Nigerian government hopes to increase the intake into secondary grammar schools from 14,000 in 1961 to 45,000 in 1970 (the Ashby Commission recommended 30,000). In May 1961 there were just over 4,000 full and part-time trainees in Nigerian government technical institutes and trade centres, while an estimated 2,700 were being trained in private industry. The Federal government's target was an output of 5,000 technicians a year and 50,000 artisans and craftsmen. This would require raising the number of teachers from 91 to 1,065, with a further 250 for commercial subjects. Mali, with only fifteen secondary schools, only one of which taught up to the *baccalauréat* standard, and a total of 3,500 pupils in mid 1961, represented a problem of a different order, and the agreement by the European Economic Community to finance a secondary school of 1,200 pupils and a teacher training college of 300 students out of its development fund constituted a major break-through.

Senegal may be taken as an example of a state in which a serious attempt has been made to meet the problem of expanding this level of education. Great emphasis is placed upon the importance of trained manpower in the development programme. As one government publication put it:

... the question of professional, industrial and agricultural training, must be considered in its technical and moral aspects as of an equivalent urgency to that of the elementary education of the masses.[10]

Even before independence, in April 1959, a State Secretariat for Technical Education and the Training of Cadres was established, and when this proved inadequate it was replaced by a Ministry in 1960. The new Ministry had five Divisions, responsible for the setting up of new establishments, the inspection of existing ones, manpower planning, and the actual creation of trained middle-grade manpower (the fifth Division was responsible for the

THE NEW STATES OF WEST AFRICA

personnel and finance of the Ministry itself). Already in existence were the Delafosse Technical College, which, with its attached schools for industrial and commercial education and correspondence courses, had about 1,500 pupils; the Saint-Louis Technical Education Group of Colleges, with 560 pupils; and the Female Apprentice Centre, with over 250 pupils. During 1960 the last was expanded into the College for the Technical Education of Young Girls, and five new establishments were founded. These were the National School of Rural Cadres, with a first group of fifty-eight students; the National School of Public Works, which was to train administrators and supervisors for both public and private engineering concerns; an Agricultural Centre for training teachers of agriculture, starting with seventy-five pupils; the Professional Centre for Training and Improvement, with courses for those who had never been to school and wished to acquire a technical skill, or who wished to improve their skills; and the National Centre for Training and Action. This last, at Rufisque, was to give courses to those who were to be the local agents of 'animation' under the Plan; in the first year over 1,000 people took these courses, including 700 teachers, and others from the Ministries of Development, Rural Economy, Finance, the Interior, Information, the Public Service, Youth and Sports, and Public Works.

If Senegal provides an example of serious planning to meet the problem of the middle-grade manpower shortage, Nigeria gives a clue to the difficulties involved with its need to find almost 1,000 technical and trade teachers if its target is to be reached. For the forseeable future the great majority of these must be recruited from abroad, and this is an expensive undertaking. Trained middle-grade manpower must be produced, and relatively it represents an even scarcer commodity than university graduates. Whether enough teachers can be found to produce a sufficient quantity of such men and women, trained to a high enough quality, is a matter for some doubt and considerable concern.

The biggest quantitative increase will be in those with only primary school education. It has already been seen that popular pressure for more schools, itself largely the result of the campaigns of the nationalists, is now exerted upon the new rulers, and that they ignore it at their own peril. A basic education for all would be a most desirable goal, were it not that at this end of the employment scale the demand for jobs far exceeds the supply, thus reversing the high- and middle-grade manpower position. Almost every educated youth expects to get a job, usually in a town, which demands the skills of literacy and does not require manual labour. As a Western Nigerian Government White Paper somewhat censoriously remarked:

Educated youths usually have strong disinclination for manual jobs and particularly farm work. They prefer soft jobs and this attitude worsens the unemployment situation.[11]

Life in the village has little attraction for most of the young people who have had any education at all. Growing populations and the resultant shortage of good farmland, the effects of traditional systems of inheritance, the irksomeness of custom to the adventurous, the attractions of town-life, with its cinemas and bars, all these combine to draw young men and women away from the rural areas. The young West African on leaving school usually expects to find a job for which literacy is a special qualification: this is true even of southern Nigeria, where by 1963 perhaps seventy per cent of school-age children were being educated. Such jobs, in Nigeria as elsewhere, are most likely to be found in the towns, and so the young Nigerian goes there and wanders about looking for employment, lodging where he can, eating when he can, haunting offices for a vacancy. Often he finally takes any job he can find, even if it is only as a labourer, but resort to crime is also frequent and suicide not uncommon.

The problem is that even in an expanding economy jobs in the non-agricultural sectors are not increasing rapidly enough to keep pace with the demand of the newly-educated. In Ghana an estimated 105,000 new jobs were created during the years 1955–61, but in the same period 164,500 young people left the primary schools, and 848,000 in all reached the age of fifteen. In Eastern Cameroun preparatory work for the Development Plan launched in December 1960 indicated that 180,000 out of an estimated potentially active male population of 828,000 were unemployed. In Nigeria it has been estimated that about 261,000 young people left school in 1961, of whom perhaps 50,000 would go on to some sort of further education, leaving over 200,000 looking for work. This is not an isolated event, but an annual one. The problem also exists in those countries which are still not within sight of universal primary education. The comparative few who are educated move to the towns in search of work, but the supply of jobs cannot meet the demand because the economy is not expanding rapidly enough. There are unemployed youths in Bamako and Porto Novo as well as in Accra or Lagos; no one knows how many. (The Nigerian National Manpower Board hoped to undertake a survey in selected towns during 1963.) If revolutions come in West Africa, it is from this group that they will draw their rank and file.

How is this problem, this serious wastage of manpower and possible political menace to be met? One drastic answer would be to halt the expansion of primary, and increase the amenities for other education. Priority has hitherto been given to quantity, to the expansion of primary education rather than secondary. Thus the C.P.P. government of the Gold Coast/Ghana made primary education free in 1952 and compulsory in 1961, but only hopes to make secondary education free by 1977. Throughout West Africa very few children receive more than a primary education; even in Ghana the number was only about thirty per cent during 1963. Yet it may be argued that it is the more highly educated young men and women who are most needed to implement the ambitious programmes of economic development adopted by most of the new states.

It is doubtful, however, if even the strongest régimes could risk the popular outcry which would follow an attempt to curtail primary education. Most governments are in fact pinning their hopes on the success of their development plans and the creation of more jobs, even if these are only unskilled ones which youths with primary education will be forced to take by necessity. Nevertheless, it is not enough to talk of creating new jobs, and the undertaking itself is a difficult one. The Plan for Eastern Cameroun, to cite one example, contained only enough industrial projects to absorb eighty-nine highly-skilled and 887 other workers in five years, and all its projects together would have given direct employment to only some 15,000 people. Modern industrialization is usually sparing in its demands for labour, and as workers acquire new skills and increase their productivity they are likely to be reduced in numbers rather than increased. This has been the experience, for instance, of the Alucam aluminium smelting plant at Edéa, in Eastern Cameroun. Moreover, if reliance is to be placed on public, rather than private, enterprise to provide new jobs, massive investment by the State will be necessary.

One widely adopted method of dealing with unemployment among the young has been the institution of schemes for 'civic service', by which young men and women are employed by the State for a limited period and set to work on public projects, while at the same time being taught some skill and, if they are illiterate, how to read and write. Such schemes have been adopted in Mali, the Ivory Coast, and Niger; there are national construction schemes in Dahomey; and Ghana and Togo have their Workers' Brigades. In some countries – Mali, for example – such schemes are combined with military training. There are, however, a number of serious obstacles to the success of such schemes. First of all, they are expensive. A proposed scheme for Eastern Cameroun was dropped for this reason. Secondly, the lack of money makes it impossible for civic service to absorb large numbers of people. Thus the Mali project covered only 3,000 volunteers in its first two years (1961–3), and the Ivory Coast government called only 2,000 young men for national service in 1961. Thirdly, such schemes are difficult to organize and administer. Their establishment can lead to the sort of administrative overlap and confusion already discussed in Chapter 4. Thus in Mali the organization of civic service involved not only the ruling party but also three different Ministries – those of the Interior and Defence, Rural Economy and the Plan, and Health and Education – as well as the Office of the High Commissioner for Youth and Sports.

In the last resolve the answer to the problem of unemployment probably lies not in the direct intervention of the State but rather in what some of the French-speaking countries term 'rural animation'. People must be shown how they can help themselves, and in particular the West African governments must help create a class of educated farmers. In Eastern and Western Nigeria, for example, farm settlements are being established and manned by educated people, who it is hoped will quickly be able to show their fellows that agriculture, using modern techniques, can be both materially and mentally rewarding. The numbers involved are relatively small, a maximum of about 5,000 farmers in the East and 7,000 in the West, but the intention is that they should set an example which others will follow on their own initiative. A programme of collective farms was launched in Dahomey during 1961. Under the Malian Plan villages are to be grouped into 'Zones of Rural Expansion', each with a seasonal school and attached farm, where selected young peasants are to be taught new methods, and then sent home with a pair of oxen, a cart, and a plough, given on credit. Each Zone is also to undertake adult education among the local farmers.

Even if sufficiently large numbers of literate young men and women can be persuaded to remain in the rural areas – and the establishment of rural industries may help here – many of the underlying problems will still remain. Populations will continue to grow, so that new jobs will continually have to be created. The other pressing need, for high and middle-grade manpower, will persist. In the end the only solution lies in the attempt to transform the economies of the West African countries by making them produce more efficiently and by diversifying them. Can the secondary and technical schools and universities produce enough trained men and women to carry out this transformation? Can the revolution in education which is now taking place in the West African countries be matched by an agrarian revolution which will ensure a decent life for the peasant farmers, more and more of whom will be literate? These are the basic questions which must be answered by the new rulers of West Africa.

7 Foreign Relations

In May 1961 a member of the Mauritanian National Assembly remarked during a debate there that 'International policy is a luxury of rich countries'. Nevertheless, it is a luxury which all must afford. The attainment of political independence by the countries of West Africa has necessarily involved them in a whole series of foreign relations at different levels, not only the special relations still usually maintained with the former metropolitan Power but also relations with other countries of the 'Western' bloc, with other independent African states, both within and outside West Africa, with other 'under-developed' countries and, in some cases, with the Communist states. Lastly, they have been called upon to play a part in the United Nations Organization and its numerous international agencies, such as the World Health Organization or the Food and Agriculture Organization. The pattern of relations which emerged in the early 1960s was a complex one, and it can probably best be understood if these first few years of independence are seen as marked by the exploring of possibilities and the tentative taking up of positions, with the positions becoming ever more clearly defined as the possibilities were more fully tested. As will be shown at the end of this chapter, it would appear that the conference held at Addis Ababa in May 1963 in fact marked the end, on more than one level, of this first phase in the evolution of the foreign relations of the West African states.

The West African States Take the Stage
The future foreign relations of these states began to emerge, in certain respects, even before independence was attained, for the

nationalist movement in each separate territory was not altogether self-contained. One political party, the R.D.A., embraced
all the French-speaking territories, and though the same was not
true of British West Africa, the political leaders in the area had
contacts with one another, made as students in Britain or the
U.S.A. and fostered by meetings such as the Pan-African Conference held at Manchester in 1945. Their opposition to colonialism also involved the West African leaders in relations with
countries outside tropical Africa which had quite recently gained
their independence, particularly those of North Africa and South
East Asia. Thus West Africans attended the Bandung Conference of April 1955. One observer has noted that 'Although
Bandung was billed as an Afro-Asian Conference, its African
voice was mainly Arab'.[1] Nevertheless, delegates from Ethiopia
did attend, as well as observers from the Gold Coast, and the
news spread widely of a common bond between peoples who had
suffered, and peoples who still suffered, from the evils of
colonial rule. The People's Republic of China was invited, the
U.S.S.R. was not; at last the non-white peoples seemed to be
coming together.

Such themes were again explored at the Afro-Asian People's
Solidarity Conference held in Cairo in January 1958, but at the
same time certain important new features emerged. First of all,
the 'Cold War' became more obtrusive; both the People's
Republic of China and the U.S.S.R. were invited to attend, and,
although the neutrality of the Afro-Asian countries was emphasized, the leader of the Soviet delegation seized the opportunity
to offer aid for development to newly-independent states.
Secondly, it became apparent that the Africans did not necessarily consider their ties with the Arab or Asian countries to be
particularly close. In March 1957, at the time of Ghana's independence, Kwame Nkrumah had already announced that he
would call a Pan-African Nationalist Conference at Accra in the
near future. After April 1958, when the first Conference of Independent African States was held at Accra, it was Ghana which
more often than not set the pace. The will of Kwame Nkrumah
towards Pan-African unity and the opportunity given him by the
comparatively early independence of Ghana ensured this central

role, which was reinforced by the holding of another meeting, the All-African People's Conference, at Accra in December 1958.

Bandung, Cairo, and the second Accra meeting of 1958 thus introduced a theme which has dominated the foreign relations of the African states, and introduced it even before most of them became independent. This theme was the solidarity of all peoples who had been subjected to colonial rule, and the need to free those who remained subjects of the 'imperialists', or, as in South Africa, of a dominant white minority. Afro-Asian Solidarity Conferences have continued to be held, at Conakry in April 1960 and Moshi (in Tanganyika) in February 1963. The first All-African People's Conference set up a permanent secretariat, the All-African People's Organization, and further Conferences have been held, at Tunis in January 1960 and Cairo in March 1961.

This first All-African People's Conference also introduced a second theme, which has dominated relations between the African states themselves. One of the resolutions stated that the 'ultimate objective of African nations is a Commonwealth of Free African States',[2] and Pan-African unity, the dream of Nkrumah and other nationalist leaders, found itself proclaimed as a goal while only a small part of the continent was free. Debate on the right way to achieve what most African leaders accepted without question as a desirable objective was to occupy much attention during the next five years.

In April 1958 there were only eight independent African states to meet in Accra, and four of these were North African.[*] After this meeting informal consultative machinery was established to coordinate policy, and in 1960 an Afro-Asian consultative committee was set up to advise the Secretary-General of the U.N.O. on developments in the former Belgian Congo.[†] The last few months of 1960 brought an even more significant development. When the Fifteenth Session of the U.N. General Assembly met in September, there were eighteen new members applying to be admitted; seventeen of them were African and sixteen of

[*] Ghana, Liberia, Ethiopia, Sudan, Egypt, Tunisia, Libya, and Morocco. The ninth, South Africa, was naturally not invited.

[†] Referred to henceforth as the Congo (Léopoldville), to distinguish it from Congo (Brazzaville), the former French Congo.

these gained admission.* The independent African states now constituted the largest single group in the General Assembly, about a quarter of its total membership, and the Afro-Asian countries together represented almost half the members. They were not slow to assert themselves. In a show of strength, they were able to force a vote of censure on the South African delegate in the General Assembly in October 1960 by sixty-seven to one, with thirty-six abstaining or otherwise not voting. The African states, most of them at this stage West African, had arrived on the international scene.

The Congo Crisis

In July 1960, before the majority of West African states had actually attained their independence, the Congo (Léopoldville) became the focal point of a world-wide crisis, and for the African states themselves this crisis raised three questions of the greatest importance. First, it spot-lighted the issue of 'neo-colonialism': to what extent could states now politically independent in fact regard themselves as their own masters? Secondly, how far was Africa to become involved in the struggle between the Western and Eastern blocs? Thirdly, were the African states going to adopt similar attitudes and policies, or would independence for a growing number of them imply division into groups within Africa itself? By February 1961 the answers to at least the second and third of these questions were quite apparent.

It was the first issue – 'neo-colonialism' – which spurred Kwame Nkrumah of Ghana and Sékou Touré of Guinea to action in July 1960. The events of 4 July to 12 July – the mutiny of the *Force Publique*, the intervention of Belgian troops, the declaration by the Katanga administration of the province's independence, and the Congolese government's request for U.N. assistance – cast doubt on the ability of the Congo (Léopoldville) to preserve its newly-attained independence. Nkrumah and

* Senegal, Mali, the Ivory Coast, Upper Volta, Dahomey, Niger, Togo, Cameroun, Gabon, Tchad, the Central African Republic, Congo (Brazzaville), Congo (Léopoldville), Madagascar, Somalia, and Nigeria were admitted. Mauritania's membership was vetoed by the U.S.S.R., for reasons given below. The non-African applicant was Cyprus.

Touré feared that the action of the Belgian government in sending troops ostensibly to protect Belgian citizens, and the involvement of Belgian business interests in the Congo's economy,
meant that Belgium, assisted by the other colonial Powers, intended to retain indirect control over the Congo, or at least over
Katanga, its richest province. As Nkrumah wrote to Patrice
Lumumba:

> Brother, we have been in the game for some time now and we know
> how to handle the imperialists and the colonialists. The only colonial-
> ist or imperialist I trust is a dead one. If you do not want to bring the
> Congo into ruin, follow the advice I have given.[3]

President Nasser of the United Arab Republic and President
Modibo Keita of Mali held the same views on Belgian motives,
and the U.A.R. was, like Ghana and Guinea, among the first to
send troops to the Congo at the request of Dag Hammarskjöld,
the U.N.O. Secretary-General.

It is significant that the three West African countries which
were most vehement in their opposition to Belgian 'neo-
colonialism' in the Congo, and which gave the strongest support
to Lumumba, were Ghana, Guinea, and Mali. In Chapter 2
these were characterized as possessing a particular type of
modern political *élite*. Although we still have a great deal to
learn about the nature of that *élite*, it is obvious that the militant
attitude of these three states stemmed from the nature of their
ruling groups and the circumstances in which they had achieved
the independence of their countries. Guinea in particular,
abruptly severed from France in 1958 and feeling, with considerable justification, that France had done its best to ensure
the collapse of the new régime, was bound to take a militantly
'anti-colonialist' line in 1960. Mali, in the latter part of that
year, was still smarting from the break-up of the Mali Federation
between itself and Senegal, and blamed this failure in part on
French intrigue. Ghana's President Nkrumah had for some time
taken an interest in Patrice Lumumba, who had attended the
All-African People's Conference in December 1958 and become
the first Prime Minister of the Congo. Ghana, however, was
rather more secure in its independence than the other two, and it
is significant that Kwame Nkrumah attempted in the early

months of the Congo crisis to act as a restraining influence upon both Lumumba and Sékou Touré.

Pressure exerted through the U.N.O. by the Afro-Asian bloc forced the withdrawal of Belgian troops by the end of July (though not from Katanga), and the presence of U.N.O. troops and technicians restored some semblance of order, at least in Léopoldville, the capital. Moise Tshombe's attempt to set up an independent state in Katanga now became the central issue, the Cold War entered Africa, and differences among the African states began to emerge. Once more, early in August, Afro-Asian pressure on the Security Council secured the passing of a motion instructing U.N. troops to enter Katanga. Belgian troops were withdrawn, but Tshombe's troops remained, stiffened with foreign mercenaries, and Dag Hammarskjöld refused to use U.N. troops to overthrow the secessionist government, as Lumumba demanded. Lumumba then turned to the U.S.S.R. and to the African states. From the U.S.S.R. he obtained lorries, technicians, transport planes, and pilots, and early in September opened the offensive against Katanga by flying troops there in ten of the aircraft. The other African states were agreed for the time being that it would be best to try and work through the United Nations Organization, and this policy was asserted at the 'Summit Meeting' of African states held in Léopoldville during the last week of August.* Guinea and the U.A.R., however, also favoured the idea of independent action by the African states to help Lumumba if the U.N. Secretary-General remained opposed to intervening in Katanga.

For a few weeks more the African states acted together to support Hammarskjöld and action through the United Nations, despite the apparent bias of the U.N. representatives against Lumumba when President Kasavubu tried to replace him by Joseph Iléo. A special session of the General Assembly met from 17–20 August and reversed the U.S.S.R.'s veto of a motion condemning any action in the Congo except through the medium of the U.N.O. Already, however, on 14 August Colonel Mobutu

* Ethiopia, Ghana, Guinea, Liberia, Libya, Morocco, Sudan, Tanganyika, Togo, Tunisia, the U.A.R., Congo (Léopoldville), and the Provisional Government of the Algerian Republic were represented.

and the Congolese army had intervened, rejected the rival claims of Lumumba and Iléo to be the legitimate Prime Minister, and established a 'College of Commissioners' instead. All Communist delegations were ordered to leave the Congo, and did so. From the end of September definite rifts appeared among the African states. The French-speaking countries of West and Equatorial Africa, with the exception of Guinea, Mali, and Togo, supported Kasavubu and Mobutu, and on 24 October they met in Abidjan to coordinate their policies. In November the U.N. General Assembly met again, to be confronted by two Congolese delegations, one representing President Kasavubu, the other Patrice Lumumba. On the twenty-second the General Assembly recognized the Kasavubu delegation as the official one with the Ivory Coast, Niger, Dahomey, Senegal, Cameroun, Gabon, Tchad, Congo (Brazzaville), and Madagascar having voted for it and Ghana, Guinea, the U.A.R., Morocco, and Togo having voted against. The Central African Republic, Ethiopia, Liberia, Libya, Somalia, Sudan, Tunisia, and Upper Volta abstained, while Nigeria took no part in the voting.

By the middle of January 1961 two groups had finally crystallized among the African states. On 15 December 1960, the French-speaking states which had gathered at Abidjan in October met again – with the addition of the Malagasy Republic – in Brazzaville. Their final communiqué declared that

> The true independence of the Congo Léopoldville requires, without doubt, that U.N.O. continues to render it its technical assistance, but it demands above all that no other State intervenes, through the medium of its soldiers or diplomats, in the internal affairs of the Congo-Léopoldville.[4]

On 4 January the Heads of State of Ghana, Guinea, Mali, Morocco, and the U.A.R., along with a delegation from Libya and an observer from Ceylon, met in Casablanca. Guinea, Mali, Morocco, and the U.A.R. had by this time abandoned all trust in the good faith of Hammarskjöld, and regarded the U.N. as a broken reed. President Nkrumah, whose personal representative had been expelled from the Congo in late November, made a final effort to persuade his friends that the U.N. should be given a last chance to support Lumumba. When it was obvious that the U.N. would not, Guinea, Morocco, and the U.A.R. announced the withdrawal of their troops from the Congo. The announcement on 13 February of Lumumba's murder in Katanga only served to set the seal on the division between the African states.

Brazzaville, Casablanca, and Monrovia

The vicissitudes of the Congo (Léopoldville) provided the occasion for a rift among the West African states almost as soon as the majority of them had become independent. Yet the Congo was not the sole source of disruption. The circumstances in which another, very different, country attained its independence also had an effect upon the foreign relations of the West African states in the early sixties. This country was Mauritania, whose right to separate independent status was challenged from the first by Morocco. As early as April 1956 the Moroccan politician Allal al-Fassi had proclaimed that Mauritania was in fact part of Morocco, and in March 1958 four Mauritanian political leaders had fled to Rabat, where they had sworn allegiance to the King of Morocco. It was in order to secure support for its claim that Morocco sought out its politically strange companions in the Casablanca Group – so-called from the conference held in January 1961 – Ghana, Guinea, Mali, and the United Arab Republic. About a month earlier Morocco had found an even stranger ally, the U.S.S.R., which in an effort to please at least one African state had vetoed Mauritania's membership of the United Nations Organization. All this naturally put Mauritania into the more moderate 'Brazzaville' camp, though Ghana had in fact recognized the new state even before the Casablanca meeting.

The nucleus of the 'moderate' camp, as has already been seen, was the group which formed itself from the majority of the French-speaking countries at the meetings in Abidjan during October and in Brazzaville during December 1960. In part the views of this group derived from a real dislike of the sort of militancy exhibited by the 'Casablanca' countries, a militancy which a man like Ahmadou Ahidjo of Cameroun, facing a Communist-supported rebellion in his own country, equated with

Communism. The reaction of Félix Houphouët-Boigny of the Ivory Coast to the Bandung Conference is revealing here. In 1959 he described it as

... the attempt of which we must be wary, for it is a spirit of hate, it severs the under-developed countries from the powers to which they were attached and finally dooms them, on the one hand to a regrouping in misery and mediocrity, on the other to a kind of perpetual auction, in which a majority of the non-committed countries live, which gives them some ephemeral successes but which cannot guarantee them the satisfaction of their constant needs.[5]

Nevertheless, the conclusion is inescapable that the conservatism of this Brazzaville Group stemmed mainly from the close relations which its member states preserved with France even after they had become politically independent. The basis of these relations was two-fold. First of all, the new ruling *élites* were genuinely attached to France and to French culture, though not always uncritically. Léopold Senghor expressed this attitude very well when he declared:

The French have their faults, I know it; they [also] have their qualities. What an admirable people and at all times deceiving, seductive, and irritating all at once. The first in Europe to form themselves into a nation, rich in virtues, engineers and soldiers, artists and workmen, the French People have the qualities of their defects. They are imperialistic, assimilationist, sentimental; they are reasonable, realistic, and humane. They strain themselves to impose their ideas and sentiments on facts. They prefer their prestige to their interests; they don't want you to love them, but to tell them that you love them. But when you resist them, when you face them with a solid dossier of facts, they end by giving in to truth – through reason and humanity.[6]

Secondly, these states had very close economic links with France, for France had reacted rapidly and effectively to the shift in the fortunes of the new Community during the second half of 1960. In April 1961 new agreements had been signed with the four Entente countries (the Ivory Coast, Dahomey, Niger, and Upper Volta), which guaranteed substantial French financial, educational, and technical help for at least the next five years, along with preferential treatment in trade. The Entente states constituted, of course, the core of the Brazzaville Group, but similar agreements were also made between France and other members of the Group.

These links with France meant that the Brazzaville countries pursued certain common policies on a number of issues which arose in the years 1960–2. They rejected Kwame Nkrumah's and Sékou Touré's fear of 'neo-colonialism'. As was seen earlier, they supported Kasavubu against Lumumba, and Mauritania against Morocco. Although they urged an early, peaceful settlement of the war in Algeria, they did not support the 'Provisional Government of the Algerian Republic' set up by the F.L.N.; some 15,000 African troops were still serving with the French army in Algeria during 1960. Houphouët-Boigny also defended the testing of atomic weapons by France in the Sahara in 1959–60.

In May 1961 the more conservative grouping widened, to include not only the Brazzaville states but also Nigeria, Liberia, Sierra Leone, Ethiopia, Togo, Libya, Tunisia, and Somalia. The countries which gathered for a conference at Monrovia did not constitute as closely knit a group as those of Brazzaville; there were differences among them on several points. Nigeria, for instance, was bitterly opposed to French atomic tests in the Sahara. But they were agreed on certain fundamental principles, and these were set out in the 'Resolution on the Means of Promoting Better Understanding and Cooperation Towards Achieving Unity in Africa and Malagasy':

1. Absolute equality of African and Malagasy States whatever may be the size of their territories, the density of their populations, or the values of their possessions;
2. Non-interference in the internal affairs of States;
3. Respect for the sovereignty of each State and its inalienable right to existence and development of its personality;
4. Unqualified condemnation of outside subversive action by neighbouring States.[7]

In these principles may be seen the crux of the opposition between the 'radical' and 'moderate' states. The latter were satisfied with the independent status they had achieved and were jealous of their newly-won sovereignty. They were (with the possible exception of Togo) content with the frontiers which they had inherited from the colonial Powers. Each dominant political *élite* wished to be left undisturbed to consolidate its position within its own country. They resented Kwame Nkrumah's attempt to assume the leadership of all West Africa, and this resentment had already been given open voice by Yussuf Maitama Sule of Nigeria at the Second Conference of Independent African States in June 1960:

... if anybody makes the mistake of feeling that he is a Messiah who has got a mission to lead Africa, the whole purpose of Pan-Africanism will, I fear, be defeated. We all can recall what Hitler thought and did in Nazi Germany and what that meant to the whole world. Hitler thought he had a mission to rule the whole world and in pursuance of his mission he tried to destroy other world Powers and plunged the whole of Europe – and indeed the whole world – into war.[8]

Not only this, but Ghana, Guinea, and Mali had proved to be havens of refuge for dissident politicians from countries like Cameroun, Niger, Togo, the Ivory Coast, and Senegal. As was noted in Chapter 5, accusations of plotting and subversion were part of the stock in trade of relations between the African states during the first few years of independence. In an insecure world these awkward neighbours made the 'Monrovia Group' of states feel even less secure.

The Casablanca states, for their part, looked with some contempt upon the others. The close ties of the conservatives with the former colonial rulers, and their ready acceptance of the apparently limited sovereignty which had been handed over to them seemed to men like Nkrumah and Sékou Touré a tribute to the strength of 'neo-colonialism' and a betrayal of the ideal of Pan-African unity. Thus, while after the Monrovia Conference Sylvanus Olympio of Togo remarked that 'At last we are beginning to think of ourselves as Africans and not simply as extensions of the European Powers', the Ghana *Evening News* referred to 'the Monrovia slave-mentality' and 'this new brand of His Master's Voice'.[9] Kwame Nkrumah in particular believed that African unity could not be achieved unless the new states began immediately to form a political union, and in this spirit he had himself stimulated the Ghana-Guinea Union in November 1958.

THE NEW STATES OF WEST AFRICA

The Casablanca Conference did not endorse his views, deciding only to set up a Political Committee to coordinate policy, an Economic Committee, a Cultural Committee, and a common military High Command. Then, in July 1961, the West African members of the group, Ghana, Guinea, and Mali, announced that they had formed the Union of African States. But although an African Common Market and an economic development bank were envisaged, and a woman member of the Mali National Assembly visiting the Ghana National Assembly early in 1962 was invited by the Speaker to 'take your rightful place among your colleagues', the Union of African States in fact failed to develop any political institutions of its own.

It must not be thought that the Brazzaville or Monrovia states were opposed to African unity. They also accepted that unity meant strength, but believed that it should not be achieved by radical measures of political reorganization, but by a policy of respecting one another's sovereignty while at the same time co-operating in such 'functional' matters as economic development, communications, public health, and education. Thus, after a preliminary conference at Yaoundé in March 1961, the Brazza-ville Group met in September at Tananarive (Madagascar) and signed the Charter of the African and Malagasy Union. An Administrative Secretariat was to be set up in Cotonou, while the headquarters of the Common Defence Pact was to be in Ouagadougou, of the Economic Cooperation Organization in Yaoundé, and of the Posts and Telecommunications Union in Brazzaville. In January 1962 the Monrovia Group met again at Lagos (though this time without Libya and Tunisia, while Sudan withdrew in the early stages) and decided to establish a perma-nent secretariat, with bodies set up to study matters like the control of disease, labour and welfare, pest control, and the Press and information. It was also decided that the Group should constitute itself as a separate entity within the United Nations General Assembly. The larger grouping of African states had thus begun to follow the pattern set by the more homogeneous French-speaking group.

The Facts of Life

The foreign relations of the new states during their first few years of independence have been described as an exploring of possibilities and a taking up of positions. Some of this exploring and some of these positions have now been examined. What should be grasped, however, if this period is to be seen in a proper perspective, is that there was a definite limit to the amount of exploring which could be done and to the number of positions which might be assumed. We have already seen that the most pressing demand upon the new rulers of these states was the need for economic development, and this could be achieved only if there was a plentiful supply of investment capital and trained manpower. Foreign policy had to be tailored to the demands of economic development. In 1962 it was estimated that the annual inflow of capital into Africa was about $1,400,000,000 from public and $500,000,000 from private sources. It was vital to the new rulers to maintain, and indeed increase this flow, and all foreign policy had to be formulated with this in mind. At times this was openly admitted. At a conference between the 'Six' of the European Economic Community and the states of the African and Malagasy Union, held in December 1961, Jacques Rabemananjara of Madagascar declared that

... the association of the Overseas States with the European Economic Community is a political action, and it would be useless and dangerous to hide this profound truth underneath the technicality of economic mechanisms. It is political from the beginning because it confirms and strengthens our ties with Europe, and again – above all – because economic development is the number one imperative for countries like ours.[10]

Most capital and technical aid still comes from the metropolitan countries, France and Britain. France itself, as part of its re-assessment of the situation in April–May 1961, sought to persuade its citizens to remain in the service of the new states, promulgating new decrees guaranteeing the salaries and service conditions of those Frenchmen who stayed on, and also guaranteeing them employment when they finally chose to return home. In 1962 direct French aid to Africa from public funds totalled 4,341 million francs (roughly £300 million), about ninety per cent of this in grants rather than loans. Aid for technical assistance represented about a quarter of the whole. The Ivory Coast, Senegal, Mali, and Togo were now able to balance their budgets without subsidies, while Cameroun had been given a grant to cover the costs of uniting West and East Cameroun. For its own part Britain set up the Department of Technical Cooperation in July 1961 to take over the organization of technical assistance, previously handled by the Ministry of Commonwealth Relations. At the conference of Commonwealth Prime Ministers held in May 1960 it had already been decided to assist present and future African Members of the Commonwealth, and during 1961 the 'Special Commonwealth African Assistance Plan' came into operation. Britain has supplied almost all the capital, £78,750,000 in 1961–2, though contrary to French practice over half of this was given in the form of loans, not direct grants. Britain also gives scholarships – 781 to Nigeria alone between October 1960 and June 1963 – and provides technical experts to work in Africa, while India, Pakistan, Canada, and Australia are giving similar help.

Four other sources of aid have become important in the last few years. The United Nations Organization is one of these. In the two years 1961 and 1962 U.N. technical assistance to Africa represented about a third of the total given to five regions of the world. Regular assistance programmes totalled $4.6 million, while the expanded programme cost $20.1 million and provided 1,632 experts and 1,618 fellowships. Between 1959 and 1962 the Special Fund financed fifty-three projects at a cost of $42.5 million, and its total for 1963 was set at the greatly increased sum of $126,000,000. In May 1961 the Economic Commission for Africa and U.N.E.S.C.O. together launched a special $11.5 million educational programme.

The International Bank for Reconstruction and Development and the International Development Association have also been active. In April 1962 they set up a new Department of Operations for Africa (excluding the Republic of South Africa and the U.A.R.), under Pierre Moussa, the former Director of Economic Affairs and Planning for the French Overseas Territories. Between September 1961 and September 1962 loans to African countries totalled $85,000,000 (though this was less than ten per cent of the total loans given by the I.B.R.D. and I.D.A. in this period), and this money has helped to finance Ghana's Volta River project and the exploitation of Mauritania's iron ore.

The sources of such funds are 'international' in character, although the Communist states in fact play very little part in them, even in the U.N. projects (the U.S.S.R.'s contribution to the Special Fund for 1963 was fixed at only $2.97 million). Two other sources which must be mentioned are part of the 'Western' bloc. One of these is the U.S.A. itself. The Clay Committee which reported early in 1963 on U.S. aid since 1945 showed that between 1 July 1945 and 30 June 1962 the government of the U.S.A. had given aid totalling $64.6 million to the countries of French-speaking West Africa (including Cameroun) and a total of $203.6 million to Ghana, Nigeria, and Sierra Leone. Liberia had had a total of $131.5 million.*

The other 'Western' source of capital is the European Economic Community, established by the Treaty of Rome on 25 March 1957. Independence for the French West African territories did not sever their relationship with the Economic Community. All except Guinea became 'associated' countries, benefiting from the special trade relations which accompanied this status. The E.E.C. also has its own development fund, FEDOM (Fonds Européen de Développement Outre-Mer), which up to 31 May 1963 had financed 326 economic or social projects presented by members or associates; over $400 million out of a total expenditure of $437 million had gone to former French possessions, with Cameroun, for instance, receiving $43.5 million, Senegal $34.6 million, and Mali $20 million.

In July 1963 a new agreement, to cover the period 1963–8, was signed by the Six and the associates. Negotiations had been protracted, and had broken down in July 1962 over France's proposal to end the system of preferential prices paid for African produce. As compensation the associates wanted their total aid

* For purposes of comparison, Morocco, with its important airbases, had had $352,000,000 in the same period, South Viet Nam $2,441,700,000, Nationalist China (Formosa) $4,428,300,000, Britain $8,713,200,000 and France $9,438,000,000. Ghana's share of the $203.6 million given to English-speaking West Africa was $156.5 million.

for the next five years to be set at $810 million; the Six were offering $700 million. The final agreement removed duties on certain tropical products, including pineapples, coconuts, raw coffee, cocoa beans, and pepper. Prices were to be brought into line with world prices, at the latest (in the case of coffee) by 1967. Aid for the period 1963–8 was finally agreed upon at $730 million, some $230 million of which were to be used to diversify products and help keep prices competitive now that the associates were meeting other producers on a more equal basis.

In the eyes of many West Africans the association of some African states with the E.E.C. has several evil effects. In the first place, it creates a division between the English-speaking and French-speaking countries. Nigeria and Ghana are strongly opposed to association with the Economic Community, as they made plain at the Commonwealth Prime Ministers' conference in September 1962, when it appeared that Britain was going to join the Community. These two countries talk in terms of an African Common Market, and they accuse the E.E.C. of preventing its associates from developing trade contacts with their neighbours. The volume of inter state trade in West Africa is very small; in 1960 Ghana sent only 2.7 per cent of its total exports to other West African countries, and received only 5.3 per cent of its total imports from them.

There can also be little doubt that these economic links with the European Six, as well as the links with the U.S.A. and the metropolitan countries, serve to limit the range of choice in the foreign policy of the new West African states. For, despite the increasing importance of the international agencies, it is bi-lateral agreements, more especially with the former colonial Powers, which provide the great bulk of the urgently-needed capital; in 1960, for instance, multi-lateral aid to Africa totalled $146 million, and bi-lateral aid $1,227 million. The influence exerted is rarely as crude as the recent gesture of Western Germany, which refused to sign the new E.E.C. agreement unless the associates undertook not to recognize East Germany (though the proviso was only written into the minutes, not incorporated in the text itself). Nevertheless, except in extraordinary circum-stances, the new states are always likely to follow lines in their foreign policy of which the Western bloc approves. The success of their plans for economic advance, to which the future viability of these states is tied, depends on their ability to avoid a balance of payments crisis and secure enough foreign capital for development. Any highly placed politician or civil servant is therefore bound to make his decisions either consciously or unconsciously in the light of this fact. Mild flirtation with the Communist countries is possible, though not every country wants to go even this far, but a true policy of 'neutralism', which Nigeria, for instance, advocates, is difficult under the circumstances, if not impossible. A country which has to raise abroad more than half the £670 million needed for its Development Plan cannot easily appear to bite the hand most likely to feed it.

Not only material factors, but cultural ones as well dispose the leaders of the new states to favour the West. As was shown earlier, the rulers of most of the French-speaking states have been closely bound to France by the ideas and habits which they absorbed as part of their education under the colonial system. To a somewhat lesser extent, this is also true of the English-speaking politicians and civil servants. It is equally true of diplomats. Consideration of foreign policy, like consideration of political or economic problems, is likely to be couched in terms learned from the metropolitan country, and this, of course, is bound to affect conduct.

Thus in the first few years after independence a whole political spectrum of states appeared in West Africa. At one end was the group most closely aligned with the West, the African and Malagasy Union. In the middle were those countries, like Nigeria, which were willing to profit from trade with the Communist countries if they could, but not to commit themselves any further. Only three states sought to have any serious dealings with the Communist countries during the early 1960s. Guinea had nothing to lose after the abrupt break with France in 1958, and everything – in terms of trade, capital, and technicians – to gain. Mali's break with France was never as complete, but her leaders were ideologically disposed to make contact with the Communist states. Ghana's leaders were similarly disposed, committed to 'a policy of neutral non-alignment, but not of passivity', and Ghana was wealthy enough by African standards to permit itself the luxury of cultivating a wide range of friendships.[11] Nevertheless, despite the hysterical pronouncements of some Western commentators, Communist influence has gained very little ground in West Africa since independence. The attempt of the U.S.S.R. to take its turn at fishing in the troubled waters of the Congo (Léopoldville) only resulted in the expulsion of its representatives by Colonel Mobutu. Similarly, an attempt by the Soviet ambassador to dabble in the internal politics of Guinea resulted in his expulsion during November 1961. Trade and aid agreements worth a total of some £100,000,000 had been made by Ghana with the U.S.S.R. and other Communist countries by the beginning of 1962, but these in no way committed the new state to any political posture in the Cold War. Instead both Guinea and Ghana have been able to benefit from the reaction of the United States to such contacts; in January 1962 the U.S.A. undertook to lend Guinea three-quarters of the capital needed for current development projects, and the United States government is contributing a substantial part of the cost of Ghana's Volta River project.

Addis Ababa – the end of the first phase?

Although the exploring of possibilities by the new states in the first years of independence led to the gradual evolution of two groups, that of Casablanca and that of Monrovia, it had become apparent by mid 1963 that this was not to be a permanent state of affairs. Neither group was very close-knit. The Monrovia Group had within it the division between English- and French-speaking countries produced by years of colonial rule. This gap, however, was gradually being bridged by various 'functional' agreements. In November 1961, for example, President Hamani Diori of Niger visited Nigeria, and agreement was reached in principle on cooperation in such matters as health, veterinary services, customs, and posts and telegraphs. Similarly, a conference on the future development of the River Niger was held at Niamey in February 1963, attended by the Ivory Coast, Dahomey, Guinea, Upper Volta, Niger, Tchad, and Nigeria. Discussions have also been held on the development of the Lake Chad basin. The Monrovia Group had the advantage of a nucleus in the African and Malagasy Union, which itself had a nucleus in the Entente Group of the Ivory Coast, Dahomey, Upper Volta, and Niger. Yet even among these last states, one, Upper Volta, made restless by its financial dependence upon remittances from the Ivory Coast, occasionally tried to assert its individuality. This culminated in a ceremonial meeting between Presidents Yaméogo and Nkrumah at Paga, on the frontier between Upper Volta and Ghana, in July 1961, when it was officially announced that there would henceforth be no restrictions on travel between the two countries, or on the transport of goods. The following month the Heads of State of the Entente group met at Abidjan, and in their final communiqué proclaimed:

> At no time have undertakings of a political nature been made by [Upper Volta] with regard to Ghana. At no time has Upper Volta envisaged leaving the Council of the Entente to which it remains faithfully joined, since this appears to be the most elastic formula in permitting each member State to maintain its cooperation with its partners on a level of perfect equality, without ever renouncing its own particular individuality.[12]

President Yaméogo had evidently been brought to heel by the economic facts of life in his poor land-locked country.

The Casablanca Group also contained divisions within it, not only between English- and French-speaking states but also between Black Africa and Arab Africa. It was the former division, however, which had become apparent by mid 1963. For more than a year before this there had been signs that Guinea was ready to seek a *rapprochement* with France. In March 1962 General de Gaulle had at last concluded the Evian agreement with the Algerian rebels, resulting in independence for Algeria, and Sékou Touré's immediate reaction was to announce a change of attitude towards the French government. In November 1962 negotiations were initiated, and at last a series of agreements was signed on 22 May 1963. These provided for the training of Guineans in France and the sending of French experts to Guinea. French assets seized by the Guinean government were released, and in return the French pensions due to Guinean ex-soldiers and civil servants, unpaid since October 1958, were to be paid.

On balance Guinea benefited immediately to the tune of some 1,500 million C.F.A. francs, while the pensions would bring another 1,000,000,000 C.F.A. francs into the country each year. In a Press conference held after the signing of the agreements, guarantees for French investment in Guinea were promised, and it was even hinted that there might be an eventual agreement with the European Economic Community. The breach between France and Guinea had been greatly narrowed, and there can be little doubt that the main reason for this was the economic difficulties which Guinea had experienced since independence, particularly the lack of foreign exchange, and the effect that this had had upon plans for development. Once again, the economic facts of life seem to have proved decisive.

Even before the Evian agreement, in February 1962, Mali had signed agreements with France granting French credits for the Malian development plan together with technical and educational aid. Although the introduction of the new Malian franc in July 1962 and the subsequent riot in Bamako (which was blamed on France) led to some worsening of relations, a further agreement between France and Mali in July 1963 postponed the repayment by Mali of advances from the French Treasury which would be due at the end of the year. Mali's most pressing need, however, was to heal the breach with Senegal which in August 1960 had destroyed the Mali Federation and blocked the new Mali's outlet to the sea via the Dakar–Niger railway. The need to bring imports up from Abidjan by road had proved a great economic handicap to Mali ever since. In June 1963 negotiations begun the previous December culminated in the signing of agreements re-opening the railway and a ceremonial meeting on 22 June between Presidents Senghor and Keita.

Even before the reconciliation between Mali and Senegal, a series of state visits between Senegal, Guinea, Mali, and the Ivory Coast during 1962 had showed that the other French-speaking states were prepared to receive Guinea and Mali back into the fold. The final isolation of Ghana – this does not seem to be too strong a way of describing it – was brought about by the *coup d'état* in Togo of January 1963. On 13 January, at a time when relations between Togo and Ghana, never good, had become even more strained, with President Nkrumah accusing President Olympio of sheltering those who were plotting against his life, Olympio was assassinated by a group of officers in the Togolese army. There does not seem to have been any reason for the *coup* other than the discontent of unemployed soldiers, returned from Algeria, and of their friends in the Togolese army. There is certainly no evidence to show the complicity of Ghana. However, the political leaders of West Africa were filled with horror at what seemed a most ominous precedent, and many tended to blame Nkrumah for what had happened. His name was already linked with 'subversion', and after the *coup* he allowed Togolese opponents of Olympio, in exile in Ghana, to return home and quickly recognized the new government of President Grunitzky. Nigeria, Cameroun, Ivory Coast, Mauritania, and Guinea were equally quick to condemn what had happened. This reaction from the first four is unsurprising, but it is of great significance that Sékou Touré did not support his old ally. Indeed, on the 22 January he sent a telegram to the Ghanaian President in which he remarked:

> The recognition by Ghana of the new Togolese government before the opening of an inquiry into the events of 13 January and before the assurance that the guilty people will be punished risks acting as a new springboard to subversive intrigues in Africa.[13]

The Casablanca Group could hardly survive such a verdict.

Such was the position when the independent African states, now thirty-two in number, met at Addis Ababa, capital of Ethiopia, on 22 May 1963. This meeting, planned ever since the Lagos Conference of January 1962, did what that Conference could not; it brought together all the blocs which had emerged among the African states. The Heads of State and Government of thirty countries attended in person; only President Grunitzky (tactfully) and King Hassan II of Morocco (because President Moktar ould Daddah of Mauritania was there) sent representatives. On 26 May all signed the Charter of the Organization of African Unity, and independent Africa was formally united. The Casablanca and Monrovia Groups were to be dissolved, though the African and Malagasy Union was not – a potential source of future discord. Despite the intended creation of an Assembly of

Heads of States and Governments and a Council of Ministers, however, this was not the political union which Kwame Nkrumah had – and still – urged. It was the view of Nigeria's Sir Abubakar Tafawa Balewa which was adopted: 'African unity must be based on the sovereignty of all African countries, whatever their size, population, and social level.'[14] The 'functional' path to unity was the one to be followed, with immediate economic, social, and cultural cooperation leading to eventual political union. A 'Preparatory Economic Commission' was left to deal with these problems.

At the Addis Ababa Conference, then, Ghana found itself without the support of Guinea and Mali and with its views on African unity rejected by this, the first full assembly of independent African states. Nevertheless, the Conference's other major decisions were ones to which Ghana could wholeheartedly subscribe. The new states were now unanimously resolved that all African peoples must be free. Before the Evian agreement France's position as a colonial Power in Algeria had greatly inhibited the states of the African and Malagasy Union, closely tied as they were to the former metropolitan country. After March 1962, however, it could be claimed that France was no longer one of the colonial Powers, and attacks on colonialism could be pressed home with vigour. Moreover, the relations between certain French-speaking states, notably Senegal and Dahomey, and Portugal had been bad since 1961. At Addis Ababa the tough, uncompromising speeches came not only from men like Algeria's Ben Bella, but from Félix Houphouët-Boigny as well. A special fund was established to give aid to liberation movements in Portuguese Africa and the Republic of South Africa; it was recommended that volunteers be raised to help these movements; and a special 'Coordinating Committee', composed of Algeria, Congo (Léopoldville), Ethiopia, Guinea, Nigeria, Senegal, Tanganyika, Uganda, and the U.A.R., was set up in Dar-es-Salaam to supervise this work. The Conference demanded that diplomatic relations with Portugal and South Africa be severed, and that all harbours and airports should be closed to them. The 'allies of the colonial powers' were 'invited' to choose between their friendship for the African peoples and their support for the Powers which were oppressing these peoples. Lastly, the Conference reaffirmed its faith in the principles of the United Nations Charter, but regretted the under-representation of Africa on the Security Council and other organs, and resolved that a separate 'African Group' should be established in the U.N., preserving friendly relations with the Asian countries.

The Addis Ababa Conference marked the end of a phase in the foreign relations of the West African states. It brought all of them together in the same conference hall and produced important decisions which all accepted – for President Nkrumah signed the Charter without apparent hesitation, though presumably with some mental reservations. It resulted in the adoption of common policies towards the U.N. and its Asian members. For the first time the new states combined to serve notice on the former colonial Powers that, however close their relations might be in other respects, the West African countries could no longer tolerate French and British support for Portugal or South Africa. Seen with the wisdom of hindsight, the shifts and twists of the early 1960s, the coming-together and drifting-apart, appear to be the first reactions of the new states to sovereign independence. These reactions were governed partly by the circumstances in which independence had been attained, but mainly, it has been suggested, by certain 'facts of life' as they appeared to the new rulers. The influence exercised by the circumstances of independence might last for only a few years. The economic facts of life and the desire to see the whole of Africa free would remain influential for years to come.

8 Conclusion

In a sense there are no conclusions which can be drawn from this study. West Africa is still in a state of flux, and at any moment some event may occur which would force a re-examination of whatever tentative hypotheses have been advanced. If, for example, a new attempt upon the life of President Nkrumah should succeed, the effect upon the internal affairs of Ghana and the relations among the West African states would be incalculable. On the other hand, the fate of one person cannot affect basic economic and social facts, and events do not occur in isolation but as part of a process which is determined by such facts.

An attempt has been made in this book to show the new states as the product of a process of economic and social change. This change was brought about in large measure by the impact of European technology, European ideas, and European rule, and one of its results was to bring into being a nationalist movement which put an end to the last of these. What we have tried to examine are the characteristics of the new rulers who succeeded the colonial Powers, the situation in which they found themselves when independence had been attained, and their first reactions to this situation. To a substantial degree this situation and these reactions were governed by the policy of the withdrawing Powers, Britain and France, during the last years of their rule.

What then were Britain and France trying to do in the years after the Second World War? Britain was trying to develop political systems in its colonies which would evolve parliamentary types of government, with legislative supremacy and opposition parties which could act as alternative governments. France was attempting to create a strong union between itself and the Overseas Territories, in the belief that this would add to the glory of France and at the same time improve the condition of the colonial peoples. British policy, therefore, was on the whole pragmatic and differed from one territory to another. French policy was in contrast guided by doctrine and attempted to treat its possessions in West Africa as a whole. Both policies failed. Britain's attempt to impose the institutions and practices of parliamentary government was wrecked on the rocks of social and political reality. In the first few years of independence forms had to be brought into line with reality, both in Ghana and in Nigeria. France's approach proved equally unrealistic. The differences in the rate and nature of the processes of social and economic change in the various territories were too strong to permit French West Africa to remain a unity, especially after the *Loi Cadre* reforms had permitted political differences among the various territorial leaders to develop. These reforms showed the African leaders that power was more easily consolidated at a territorial level than on some larger scale. Moreover, the taste for power grew, so that France's final attempt to find a mutually acceptable union – the Franco-African Community – proved abortive. The separate independence of each territory was the only possible answer, although economic and cultural factors kept nearly all the territories tied closely to France.

Thus by the end of 1960 almost all the British and French possessions in West Africa were politically independent. The next step was for the new rulers to consolidate their power, although in some countries this process had begun in anticipation several years before independence. Once again differing social and economic realities determined the form taken by this struggle. The outcome in the French-speaking states was the emergence of one dominant party, which proceeded to absorb or destroy all serious or potentially serious rivals: this included not only other parties, but also pressure groups of all kinds. Although in some countries – Dahomey, for example – the struggle was bitter, this process was on the whole relatively easy. The French were not committed to a parliamentary system of government in the way that the British were, and the example of the multi-party system as it worked, or failed to work, under the Fourth Republic must have provided the African leaders with a persuasive argument. The English-speaking states – with the exception of Ghana – were slower to adopt the pattern of a single dominant party controlling all politically-significant organizations. By mid 1963, however, the opposition in Nigeria was under heavy pressure, and there was strong support at least for a period of 'national' government and a moratorium on party competition. In Sierra Leone the government of Sir Milton Margai had also shown that it was quite prepared to deal severely with the opposition, if it ever seemed necessary.

The ethics of one-party rule has occupied the attention of many politicians and commentators in the last few years, more particularly, perhaps, in the English-speaking world. Critics of the African states have far too often devoted their attention to outward forms and not to inner realities. Whether or not there is an opposition party able to provide an alternative government is not all that important; even if opposition was tolerated, such parties would not exist in any of the West African states, with the possible exception of Nigeria. The inner reality is a basic political – indeed, philosophical – question. How may a decent life be ensured for the citizens of the State, and in ensuring this decent life how may efficiency be balanced against the Rule of Law and protection from arbitrary action? The ability to reach such objectives is not a monopoly of any one form of government. Britain and the U.S.A. can afford to regard elective forms of government as ends in themselves because a decent life is assured for most (though by no means all) of their citizens by their technological superiority, natural wealth, and economic dominance over much of the rest of the world. (Moreover, the Marxist would say, this devotion to elective government is a sham anyway, since the high standard of living is in substantial measure the result of the economic exploitation of the under-developed areas.) The rulers of the new states must seek the form of government which seems to provide the most rapid solution to the problems of their poverty-stricken societies, and cannot afford to regard any one form as an end in itself.

On the other hand, no amount of argument can justify cruelty and injustice wherever they occur. Indeed, it would be an insult to the new states if outside observers did not judge them by the same standards as other political systems are judged. Imprisonment of opposition leaders without fair trial, or with no trial at all, the establishment of courts made up of politicians to try other politicians, and the retention of sedition laws which were passed in the colonial period and earned justifiable criticism then, all these arouse grave doubts about the Rule of Law and basic respect for human rights. Corruption, nepotism, and the bullying of those less powerful are offences against human decency whether they occur in West Africa or Western Europe, the U.S.A. or the U.S.S.R.

Underlying everything else in West Africa, of course, are the economic and social realities: as President Grunitzky put it in an interview in June 1963:

> Of what use would political unity be if the Togolese economic situation did not improve, if a great number of workers continued to be unemployed, if the country's budget likewise did not allow the proper running of our administrative services?[1]

These are desperately poor countries, dependent for their international livelihood upon fluctuating world markets, with growing populations to be fed, clothed, housed, and educated. Production must be increased in every sector of the economy; more men and women must be trained for every sort of job; great sums of money must be raised abroad to supplement this domestic effort. And the supply of capital is linked to the intricate question of how to be a small country in a world of great Powers, regarding one another as potential enemies in a World War. The West African states had a chilly introduction to foreign relations, for no sooner were most of them independent than they were involved in the complex Congo crisis. As one observer has written: 'Pan-Africanism met its first real challenge in the Congo: previously, the emotional urge towards continental unity had been tested only in committee rooms and on conference platforms.'[2] The Congo crisis provided an early occasion for underlying realities to assert themselves; divisions among states appeared, and the next few years saw various groupings and regroupings. This pattern will no doubt be repeated in other forms during the years to come.

Beset by economic and social problems to which solutions must be found, plunged into the rapids of world politics, the new rulers must do what they can with what they have to hand. New institutions must be evolved to perform tasks which the government has never before attempted on such a scale. Nations must be built, and unity achieved among peoples who are sometimes by no means sure that they want it. At this stage the political systems of the new states are frighteningly fragile. Political activity can still erupt into violence at a moment's notice, and as a result governments are disposed to tighten rather than relax their grip. The Senegalese government, for instance, felt it necessary to maintain a State of Emergency from the break-up of the Mali Federation in August 1960 until June 1963, and political meetings have been forbidden in Lagos, the Nigerian federal capital, almost continuously since independence was achieved in October 1960. Political crises have shaken many states since independence. Ghana suffered serious disruption from strikes in September 1961, and there have been bomb explosions and attempts on the life of the President. In November 1961 there were disputes within the ruling party of Guinea, along with student strikes and other popular demonstrations against voluntary labour. In Mali rioting in the capital during July 1962 led to the trial of prominent former leaders of the opposition to the Union Soudanaise-R.D.A. In December 1962 there was an attempted *coup d'état* in Senegal. In Togo a *coup* was successful in January 1963, and the President was assassinated. In April 1963 three former ministers, amongst others, were sentenced by a special court in the Ivory Coast for plotting with a 'Communist' organization to overthrow the government.

Economically the situation is no less precarious. Nigerian leaders publicly express their disappointment at the failure of foreign governments and private investors to come forward with the money needed for development. In Upper Volta the Council of Ministers decided in January 1963 that the Five Year Plan was unworkable, and should be replaced by an interim plan to cover the next two years; five months later a minister was arrested for embezzling public funds. In Senegal President Senghor spoke in April 1963 of the difficulties which the Development Plan was suffering, and lamented 'the atmosphere of chicanery and the clan spirit which marked the year just gone by, dealing a blow, I do not say mortal, but grave, to the plan'.[3] Everywhere popular expectation far exceeds the perceptible results of planning and investment: people notice that far too often their taxes increase but their incomes do not, that the local legislator has a new car while their children die from malaria or *kwashiorkor*.

All this lays a heavy responsibility upon many shoulders. Now that outsiders have no direct control over what happens in the West African states they have a responsibility, not to suspend all criticism, but to show some real understanding of the great problems which the new rulers face. On the other hand, it is these rulers who bear the greatest responsibility. They take decisions every day which literally mean life or death to millions of people, not the life or death decisions of those who govern the great Powers, whose weapons can blast multitudes in a few minutes, but decisions which in the next decades can mean a better life for the many now dying in poverty. This is an all but crushing burden. If the new rulers can bear it successfully, they will earn their place among the great statesmen of history. If they give way to self-interest and love of power for its own sake, the result will be certain misery, probable anarchy, and the condemnation of posterity.

Notes and Further Reading

N.B. For reasons of space the notes have been kept to a minimum, and are mainly references for quotations. The bibliography for each chapter contains other items which the author has found especially useful and interesting, but it is by no means exhaustive. There are six periodicals which supply a constant stream of news and comment, and the files of these should be consulted on any matter discussed in this book. These are *Africa Digest*, published by the Africa Publications Trust in London; *Africa Report* (known until October 1960 as *Africa Special Report*), published in Washington D.C. by the Institute of African-American Relations; *Afrique Contemporaine*, published in Paris by the Centre d'Étude et de Documentation sur l'Afrique et l'Outre-Mer; *Afrique Nouvelle*, published by the Société d'Éditions de l'Afrique Nouvelle in Dakar; *Chronologie Politique Africaine*, published in Paris by the Centre d'Étude des Relations Internationales de la Fondation Nationale des Sciences Politiques; and *West Africa*, published in London by Overseas Newspapers (Agencies) Ltd.

CHAPTER I

Notes

(1) Three works are particularly valuable: Thomas Hodgkin's *Nationalism in Colonial Africa*, London, Frederick Muller, 1956; James S. Coleman's *Nigeria: Background to Nationalism*, Berkeley and Los Angeles, University of California Press, 1958; and Dennis Austin's *Politics in Ghana, 1946–1960*, London, Oxford University Press for the Royal Institute of International Affairs, *1964*.

(2) These figures are for the mid 1930s, and in the case of French West Africa do not include Cameroun. The estimates of population should be treated with caution.

(3) *Conférence Africaine Brazzaville, 30 janvier 1944–8 février 1944*, Paris, Ministère des Colonies, 1945, p. 22.

(4) Quoted in Ernest Milcent: *L'A.O.F. entre en Scène*, Paris, Bibliothèque de l'Homme d'Action, 1958, p. 79.

(5) André Blanchet: *L'Itinéraire des Partis africains depuis Bamako*, Paris, Librairie Plon, 1958, p. 1.

Some Additional Reading

Ansprenger, Franz: *Politik im Schwarzen Afrika*, Köln und Opladen, Westdeutscher Verlag, 1961.

Berg, Elliot J.: 'The Economic Basis of Political Choice in French West Africa', *American Political Science Review*, Vol. LIV, No. 2, June 1960.

Bourret, F. M.: *Ghana: the Road to Independence, 1919–1957*, London, Oxford University Press, 1960.

Coleman, James S.: 'Togoland', *International Conciliation*, No. 509, September 1956.

Crowder, Michael: *Senegal: a Study of French Assimilation Policy*, London, Oxford University Press for the Institute of Race Relations, 1962.

Dessarre, Eve: *Quel sera le Destin de l'Afrique ?*, Paris, Librairie Plon, 1961.

Du Bois, Victor D.: 'Guinea's Prelude to Independence', American Universities Field Staff Reports Service, West Africa Series, Vol. V, No. 6 and 'The Guinean Vote for Independence', ibid., Vol V, No. 7.

Dugué, Gil: *Vers les États-unis d'Afrique*, Dakar, Éditions 'Lettres africaines', 1960.

Ezera, Kalu: *Constitutional Developments in Nigeria*, London, Cambridge University Press, 1960.

Fage, J. D.: *Introduction to the History of West Africa*, London, Cambridge University Press, 1956.

Fage, J. D., and Oliver, Roland: *A Short History of Africa*, London, Penguin African Library, 1962.

Hamon, L.: 'Introduction à l'étude des partis politiques de l'Afrique française', *Revue juridique et politique d'Outremer*, April–June 1959, and 'Le Parti fédérale africain et le Rassemblement démocratique africain de la querelle fédéraliste à l'indépendance (1959–1960)', ibid., October–December 1960, and 'II. le R.D.A.', ibid., July–September 1961, and 'Le Parti démocratique de Guinée (d'avant l'Indépendance à 1960)', ibid.

Nkrumah, Kwame: *Ghana: the Autobiography of Kwame Nkrumah*, Edinburgh, Thomas Nelson and Sons, 1957, and *I Speak of Freedom*, London, Heinemann, 1961.

Robinson, Kenneth: 'Senegal: the Elections to the Territorial Assembly, March 1957', in *Five Elections in Africa*, edited by W. J. M. Mackenzie and K. E. Robinson, Oxford, Clarendon Press, 1960.

Schachter, Ruth: *Parties of French-Speaking West Africa*, London, Oxford University Press, in press.

Schachter, Ruth, and Hodgkin, Thomas: 'French-speaking West Africa in Transition', *International Conciliation*, No. 528, May 1960.

Segal, Ronald: *Political Africa*, London, Stevens and Sons, 1961, and *African Profiles*, London, Penguin African Library, 1962.

Siriex, P-H.: *Une nouvelle Afrique*, Paris, Librairie Plon, 1957.

Thompson, Virginia, and Adloff, Richard: *French West Africa*, London, George Allen and Unwin, 1958.

Wallerstein, Immanuel: *Africa: the Politics of Independence*, New York, Vintage Books, 1961.

CHAPTER 2

Notes

(1) For a study of this phenomenon see Polly Hill's *The Gold Coast Cocoa Farmer*, London, Oxford University Press, 1956.

(2) The figure for British West Africa is only approximate, but is in the correct order of comparative magnitude.

(3) H. F. C. Smith: 'A Neglected Theme of West African History: the Islamic Revolutions of the 19th Century', *Journal of the Historical Society of Nigeria*, Vol. 2, No. 2, December 1961, pp. 169–70.

(4) A detailed discussion of this may be found in J. Spencer Trimingham's *A History of Islam in West Africa*, Oxford, Clarendon Press, 1962, pp. 20–33.

(5) Smith, op. cit., p. 170.

(6) *La Liberté*, 28 December 1954.

(7) Madeira Keita: 'Le Parti unique en Afrique', *Présence africaine*, Vol. XXX, February–March 1960, p. 21.

Some Additional Reading

Apter, David: *The Gold Coast in Transition*, Princeton, Princeton University Press, 1955.

Austin, Dennis: *Politics in Ghana, 1946–1960*, q.v.

Awolowo, Obafemi: *Awo: the Autobiography of Chief Obafemi Awolowo*, London, Cambridge University Press, 1960.

Bello, Sir Ahmadu: *My Life*, London, Cambridge University Press, 1962.

Coleman, James S.: *Nigeria: Background to Nationalism*, q.v.

Crowder, Michael: *Senegal: a Study in French Assimilation Policy*, q.v.

Delavignette, Robert: *Freedom and Authority in French West Africa*, London, Oxford University Press for the International African Institute, 1950.

Hilliard, F. H.: *A Short History of Education in British West Africa*, Edinburgh, Thomas Nelson and Sons, 1957.

Hodgkin, Thomas: *Nationalism in Colonial Africa*, q.v., and *African Political Parties*, London, Penguin Books, 1962.

Hunter, Guy: *The New Societies of Tropical Africa*, London, Oxford University Press for the Institute of Race Relations, 1962.

Kilson, Martin J.: 'The Analysis of African Nationalism', *World Politics*, Vol. X, No. 3, April 1958, and 'Nationalism and Social Classes in British West Africa', *The Journal of Politics*, Vol. XX, 1958.

Kimble, David: *A Political History of Ghana, 1850–1928*, Oxford, Clarendon Press, 1963.

Little, Kenneth: 'Structural Change in the Sierra Leone Protectorate', *Africa*, Vol. XXV, No. 3, July 1955.

Mercier, P.: 'Evolution of Senegalese Élites', *International Social Science Bulletin*, Vol. VIII, No. 3, 1956.*

Mumford, W. Bryant, and Orde-Brown, G. St. J.: *Africans Learn to be French*, London, Evans Brothers, n.d.

Nkrumah, Kwame: *Ghana: the Autobiography of Kwame Nkrumah*, q.v.

Perham, Margery: *Native Administration in Nigeria*, London, Oxford University Press, 1937.

Porter, A. T.: *Creoledom: a Study of the Development of Freetown Society*, London, Oxford University Press, 1963.

Post, K. W. J.: *The Nigerian Federal Election of 1959*, London, Oxford University Press for the Nigerian Institute of Social and Economic Research, 1963.

Schachter, Ruth: *Parties of French-Speaking West Africa*, q.v.

Schachter, Ruth, and Hodgkin, Thomas: 'French-speaking West Africa in Transition', q.v.

Seurin, J-L.: 'Élites sociales et Partis politiques d'A.O.F.', *Annales africaines*, 1958.

Smith, M. G.: *Government in Zazzau*, London, Oxford University Press for the International African Institute, 1960.

* The whole issue was devoted to the theme 'African *Élites*'.

Trimingham, J. Spencer: *Islam in West Africa*, Oxford, Clarendon Press, 1959.

Wallerstein, Immanuel: *Africa: the Politics of Independence*, q.v.

Wise, Colin G.: *A History of Education in British West Africa*, London, Longmans, Green and Co., 1956.

CHAPTER 3

Notes

(1) For a discussion of this problem of conceptualization see Father J O'Connell: 'Senghor, Nkrumah and Azikiwe: Unity and Diversity in the West African State', *The Nigerian Journal of Economic and Social Studies*, Vol. 5, No. 1, March 1963.

(2) L. S. Senghor: 'Rapport sur la Doctrine et le Programme du Parti', *Nation et Voie Africaine du Socialisme*, Paris, Présence africaine, 1961, pp. 22–3.

(3) ibid., page 23.

(4) *Senegal Magazine*, Special Independence Celebrations Number, April–May 1961.

(5) Mamadou Dia: *The African Nations and World Solidarity*, translated by Mercer Cook, New York, Frederick A. Praeger, 1961, p. 5.

(6) *Proceedings and Report of the Commission Appointed to Inquire into the Matters disclosed at the Trial of Captain Benjamin Awhaitey before a Court-Martial and the Surrounding Circumstances*, Accra, Government Printer, 1959, p. 478.

(7) See John P. Mackintosh: 'The Nigerian Federal Parliament', *Public Law*, Autumn 1963.

(8) L. S. Senghor, op. cit. p. 23.

(9) *Fraternité*, 22 May 1959, quoted in L. Hamon: 'Le Parti fédérale africain et le Rassemblement démocratique africain de la querelle fédéraliste à l'indépendance (1959–1960). II. le R.D.A.', q.v., p. 344.

(10) L. S. Senghor: 'La Voie africaine du Socialisme', *Nation et Voie africaine du Socialisme*, pp. 125–6.

(11) See Lester N. Trachtman: 'The Labor Movement of Ghana: a Study in Political Unionism', *Economic Development and Cultural Change*, Vol. X, No. 2, Part 1, January 1962.

(12) See J-L. Seurin: 'Élites sociales et Partis politiques d'A.O.F.', q.v.

(13) *Fraternité*, 7 August 1959, quoted in Hamon, op. cit. p. 345.

Some Additional Reading

Austin, Dennis: *Politics in Ghana, 1946–1960*, q.v.

Bretton, Henry L.: *Power and Stability in Nigeria*, New York, Frederick A. Praeger, 1962.

Carter, Gwendolen M. (edit.): *African One-Party States*, Ithaca, Cornell University Press, 1962.

Du Bois, Victor D.: 'The Problems of Independence', American Universities Field Staff Reports Service, West Africa Series, Vol. V, No. 8.

Hodgkin, Thomas: *African Political Parties*, q.v., and 'A Note on the Language of African Nationalism' in *African Affairs, Number One*, St Anthony's Papers Number 10, London, Chatto & Windus, 1961.

Keita, Madeira: 'Le Parti unique en Afrique', q.v.

Kilson, Martin J.: 'Authoritarian and Single-Party Tendencies in African Politics', *World Politics*, Vol. XV, No. 2, January 1963.

Kouame, S.: 'La vie parlementaire ivoirienne ou l'absence de rivalités idéologiques', *Penant*, No. 689, 1961.

Mackintosh, John P.: 'Electoral Trends and the Tendency to a One Party System in Nigeria', *Journal of Commonwealth Political Studies*, Vol. I, No. 3, November 1962, and 'Politics in Nigeria: the Action Group Crisis of 1962', *Political Studies*, Vol. XI, No. 2, June 1963.

Nkrumah, Kwame: *I Speak of Freedom*, q.v., and *Africa Must Unite*, London, Heinemann, 1963.

Potekhin, I.: 'The Formation of Nations in Africa', *Marxism Today*, Vol. II, No. 10, October 1958.

Rosberg, Carl G.: 'Democracy and the New African States', *African Affairs, Number Two*, St Anthony's Papers Number 15, London, Chatto and Windus, 1963.

Schachter, Ruth: *Parties of French-Speaking West Africa*, q.v., and 'Single Party Systems in West Africa', *American Political Science Review*, Vol. LV, No. 2, June 1961.

Wallerstein, Immanuel: *Africa: the Politics of Independence*, q.v., and 'Ethnicity and National Integration in West Africa', *Cahiers d'Études africaines*, Vol. I, No. 3, October 1960.

Zang Atangana, J-M.: 'Les Partis politiques camerounais', *Penant*, No. 684, December 1960.

CHAPTER 4

Notes

(1) *Senegal Magazine*, Special Independence Number, 4 April 1962,

p. 7. 'Symbiosis' is defined by the *Concise Oxford Dictionary*, Fourth Edition, 1951, as a 'permanent union between organisms each of which depends for its existence on the other'.

(2) See, for example, J. Buchmann: 'La tendance au présidentialisme dans les nouvelles constitutions négro-africaines', *Civilisations*, Vol. XII, No. 1, 1962, and L. Dubouis: 'Le régime présidentiel dans les nouvelles constitutions des États africains d'expression française', *Penant*, No. 691, April–May 1962.

(3) See John P. Mackintosh: 'The Nigerian Federal Parliament', q.v.

(4) *L'Essor hebdomadaire*, 3 June 1960.

(5) ibid., 10 June 1960.

(6) See L. Gray Cowan: *Local Government in West Africa*, New York, Columbia University Press, 1958.

(7) *Communication du Ministre de l'Intérieur sur la Réforme administrative et Discours prononcé à l'occasion de la réunion des Chefs d'Arrondissement à Dakar*, Saint Louis, Imprimerie de la République du Sénégal, 1960, p. 7.

(8) ibid., p. 18.

(9) ibid., p. 7.

(10) *L'Essor hebdomadaire*, 10 June 1960.

(11) ibid.

(12) This instance is quoted in an article by Bernard Charles, 'Un Parti Politique Africain. Le Parti Démocratique de Guinée', *Revue française de Science politique*, Vol. XII, No. 2, June 1962.

(13) *L'Essor hebdomadaire*, 3 June 1960.

Some Additional Reading

de Béthune, E., and Wembi, A.: 'Le problème de la sous-administration dans les pays d'Afrique noire indépendante', *Civilisations*, Vol. XII, No. 4, 1962.

Carter, Gwendolen M. (edit.): *African One-Party States*, q.v.

Césaire, Aimé: 'La pensée politique de M. Sékou Touré, *Présence africaine*, New Series, Vol. XXIX, December 1959–January 1960.

Cole, Taylor: 'Bureaucracy in Transition' in *The Nigerian Political Scene*, edited by Robert O. Tilman and Taylor Cole, Durham N.C., Duke University Press, 1962.

Du Bois, Victor D.: 'The Party and the Government', American Universities Field Staff Reports Service, West Africa Series, Vol. V, No. 2.

Fischer, G.: 'Quelques aspects de la doctrine politique guinéenne', *Civilisations*, Vol. IX, No. 4, 1959.

Gigon, Fernand: *Guinée: État-pilote*, Paris, Librairie Plon, 1959.

Muracciole, Luc (edit.): *Les Constitutions des États africains d'Expression française*, Paris, Librairie générale de Droit et de Jurisprudence, 1961.

Nkrumah, Kwame: *I Speak of Freedom*, q.v., and *Africa Must Unite*, q.v.

Robinson, Kenneth: 'Constitutional Autochthony in Ghana', *Journal of Commonwealth Political Studies*, Vol. I, No. 1, November 1961.

Rubin, Leslie, and Murray, Pauli: *The Constitution and Government of Ghana*, London, Sweet and Maxwell, 1961.

Touré, Sékou: *Expérience guinéenne et Unité africaine*, Paris, Présence africaine, n.d.

Wallerstein, Immanuel: 'L'Idéologie du P.D.G.', *Présence africaine*, Vol. XL, First Quarter, 1962.

Zolberg, Aristide R.: 'Effets de la structure d'un parti politique sur l'intégration nationale', *Cahiers d'Études africaines*, Vol. I, No. 3, October 1960.

'The Administrative Machinery of the New States', editorial, *Civilisations*, Vol. XII, No. 4, q.v.

'L'Action Politique du P.D.G.', *Conférences Hebdomadaires*, Tome IX, Conakry: n.p., n.d.

What are the Problems of Parliamentary Government in West Africa?, London, the Hansard Society, 1958.

CHAPTER 5

Notes

(1) 'Towards Nkrumaism: the Building of Socialist Ghana', *Report on Doctrine and Orientation presented by John K. Tettegah, Secretary-General of the Ghana T.U.C. to the First Biennial Congress held at Kumasi, 26th–30th March, 1962*, Accra, Education and Publicity Department of the T.U.C. (Ghana), mimeographed, n.d., p. 1.

(2) Madeira Keita: 'Le Parti unique en Afrique', q.v., p. 9.

(3) *Draft Programme of the Convention People's Party for Work and Happiness*, Accra: Ministry of Information and Broadcasting, n.d., p. 4.

(4) *Address by Osagyefo Dr Kwame Nkrumah at the Eleventh Party Congress at Kumasi on 29th July, 1962*, Accra: Ministry of Information and Broadcasting, n.d., p. 5.

(5) See Table 29 on p. 160 of S. Herbert Frankel's *Capital Investment in Africa*, London, Oxford University Press, 1938.

(6) *Draft Programme of the Convention People's Party for Work and Happiness*, q.v., p. 5.

(7) *Federation of Nigeria National Development Plan 1962–68*, Lagos, the Federal Ministry of Economic Development, n.d., p. 3.

(8) *Draft Programme of the Convention People's Party for Work and Happiness*, q.v., p. 15.

(9) *Rapport sur le Plan quinquennal de Développement économique et social de la République du Mali, 1961–1965*, Bamako, Ministère du Plan et de l'Économie rurale, n.d., p. 7.

(10) For a seminal discussion of entrepreneurial activity and economic development see W. W. Rostow: 'The Take-off into Self-Sustained Growth', the *Economic Journal*, March 1956.

(11) *Chronologie politique africaine*, second year, No. 4, July–August 1961, p. 12.

(12) *Draft Programme of the Convention People's Party for Work and Happiness*, q.v., p. 15.

(13) *Chronologie politique africaine*, second year, No. 5, September–October 1961, p. 23.

(14) *Federation of Nigeria National Development Plan 1962–68*, p. 21.

(15) *Sénégal Faits et Chiffres*, Dakar: Services de Presse du Ministère de l'Information, de la Presse, et de la Radiodiffusion, 1962, pp. 26–7.

(16) *Rapport sur le Plan quinquennal de Développement économique et social de la République du Mali, 1961–1965*, q.v., p. 21.

(17) *Federation of Nigeria National Development Plan 1962–68*, q.v., p. 5.

(18) *Rapport sur le Plan quinquennal de Développement économique et social de la République du Mali, 1961–1965*, q.v., p. 8.

Some Additional Reading

Bauer, P.: *West African Trade*, London, Cambridge University Press, 1954.

Berg, Elliot J.: 'The Economic Basis of Political Choice in French West Africa', q.v.

Du Bois, Victor D.: 'Reorganization of the Guinean Economy', American Universities Field Staff Reports Service, West Africa Series, Vol. VI, No. 1.

Dumont, René: *L'Afrique noire est mal partie*, Paris, Éditions du Seuil, 1962.

Garlick, Peter: *African Traders in Kumasi*, Accra, University College of Ghana Economic Research Division, 1959, and 'African and Levantine Trading Firms in Ghana', *Nigerian Institute of Social and Economic Research Conference Proceedings*, December 1960, Ibadan, the Institute, n.d.

Green, R. H.: 'Ghana Cocoa Marketing Policy 1938–60', ibid.

Hill, Polly: *The Gold Coast Cocoa Farmer*, q.v.

Hunter, Guy: *The New Societies of Tropical Africa*, q.v.

Krantz-Grandmougin, J.: *Mali*, Bamako, Chamber of Commerce, Agriculture, and Industry, October 1961.

Moussa, Pierre: *The Underprivileged Nations*, London, Sidgwick and Jackson, 1962.

Nkrumah, Kwame: *Africa Must Unite*, q.v.

Sutton, Francis X.: 'Planning and Rationality in the Newly Independent States in Africa', *Economic Development and Cultural Change*, Vol. X, No. 1, October 1961.

Thompson, Virginia, and Adloff, Richard: *French West Africa*, q.v.

Tixier, G.: 'Les finances publiques et la politique budgétaire des États de l'Afrique de l'Ouest', *Penant*, No. 691, April–May 1962.

A.O.F. 1957: Tableaux économiques, Dakar, Haut Commissariat de la République en Afrique Occidentale Française, 1958.

'Basic Data on the Economy of the Republic of Guinea', *U.S. Department of Commerce World Trade Information Service Economic Reports Part I*, No. 60–35, August 1960.

'Basic Data on the Economy of Sierra Leone', ibid., No. 62–80, November 1962.

'Economic Developments in the Republic of Guinea 1961', ibid., No. 62–62, August 1962.

Economic Survey of Africa since 1950, New York, United Nations Department of Economic and Social Affairs, 1959.

'Encadrement rural en République du Mali', *Action Rurale*, Édition spéciale, Bamako, Ministère du Plan et de l'Économie rurale, n.d.

L'Investissement Humain dans le Développement Socialiste, Dakar: Commissariat général au Plan, Bureau d'Études, April 1962, mimeographed, unpublished.

Note sur la Planification de l'Évolution structurelle et le Développement socialiste, Dakar, Présidence du Conseil, August 1962, mimeographed, unpublished.

'Organisation du Monde rural en République du Mali', *Action Rurale*, Édition spéciale, Bamako, Ministère du Plan et de l'Économie rurale, n.d.

Rapport sur la première année de l'Exécution du Plan quadriennal 1961–1964 de la République du Sénégal, Dakar: Commissariat général au Plan, June 1962, mimeographed, unpublished.

République du Mali Données Économiques, Bamako, Ministère du Plan et de l'Économie rurale, n.d.

Le Sénégal en marche, Dakar, Services de Presse du Ministère de l'Information, de la Presse, et de la Radiodiffusion, 1961.
Senegal Magazine, Special Independence Number, 4 April 1962, q.v.

CHAPTER 6

Notes

(1) *Republic of Ghana First Seven-Year Development Plan* (draft), Accra, Office of the Planning Commission, March 1963, mimeographed, unpublished, Chapter 7, p. 1. (N.B. The draft version numbered the pages of each chapter separately.)

(2) René Dumont: *L'Afrique noire est mal partie*, q.v., p. 80.

(3) *Republic of Ghana First Seven-Year Development Plan*, Chapter 2, p. 10.

(4) See, for instance, Dumont, op. cit., p. 191.

(5) Obafemi Awolowo: *Awo: the Autobiography of Chief Obafemi Awolowo*, q.v., p. 27.

(6) *Republic of Ghana First Seven-Year Development Plan*, Chapter 7, p. 3.

(7) Guy Hunter: *The New Societies of Tropical Africa*, q.v., p. 246.

(8) *Le Sénégal en marche*, q.v., p. 158.

(9) *Republic of Ghana First Seven-Year Development Plan*, Chapter 1, p. 6.

(10) *Le Sénégal en marche*, p. 157.

(11) *White Paper on Integrated Rural Development*, Western Nigeria Official Document No. 8 of 1963, Annexure 1, p. 1.

Some Additional Reading

Balima, Salfo Albert: 'Notes on the Social and Labour Situation in the Republic of Upper Volta', *International Labour Review*, Vol. LXXXII, No. 4, October 1960.

Bispham, W. M. L.: 'Middle Grade Non-Technical Officials and Management in Nigeria, with Particular Reference to the Federal Territory and Western Nigeria', unpublished paper, February 1961.

Callaway, Archibald: 'School Leavers and the Developing Economy of Nigeria', in *The Nigerian Political Scene*, edited by Robert O. Tilman and Taylor Cole, q.v.

Cole, Taylor: 'Bureaucracy in Transition', ibid.

Fraisse, André: 'Étude sur la formation des cadres moyens au Mali', unpublished paper, November 1961.

Harbison, Frederick H.: 'Human Resources and Economic Development in Nigeria', *The Nigerian Political Scene*, q.v., and 'Human

Resources Development Planning in Modernising Economies', *International Labour Review*, Vol. LXXXV, No. 5, May 1962.

Hilliard, F. H.: *A Short History of Education in British West Africa*, q.v.

Kitchen, Helen (edit.): *The Educated African*, London, Heinemann, 1962.

Mumford, W. Bryant, and Orde-Brown, G. St J.: *Africans Learn to be French*, q.v.

O'Connell, J.: 'The State and the Organisation of Elementary Education in Nigeria, 1945–60', unpublished essay, n.d.

Spengler, Joseph J.: 'Population Movements and Economic Development in Nigeria', *The Nigerian Political Scene*, q.v.

Sutton, Francis X.: 'Planning and Rationality in the Newly Independent States in Africa', q.v.

Thompson, Virginia, and Adloff, Richard: *French West Africa*, q.v.

Wise, Colin G.: *A History of Education in British West Africa*, q.v.

Yesufu, T. M.: 'Nigerian Manpower Problems (a Preliminary Assessment)', *The Nigerian Journal of Economic and Social Studies*, Vol. 4, No. 3, November 1962.

Younger, Kenneth: *The Public Service in the New States*, London, Oxford University Press, 1960.

'Economic Development and Employment in Eastern Cameroun', *International Labour Review*, Vol. LXXXV, No. 6, June 1962.

'Encadrement rural en République du Mali', *Action Rurale*, q.v.

Federation of Nigeria National Development Plan, 1962–68, q.v.

L'Investissement Humain dans le Développement Socialiste, q.v.

Investment in Education: the Report of the Commission on Post-School Certificate and Higher Education in Nigeria, Lagos, Federal Ministry of Education, 1960.

'Organisation du Monde rural en République du Mali', *Action Rurale*, q.v.

Rapport sur le Plan quinquennal de Développement économique et social de la République du Mali, 1961–1965, q.v.

Sénégal Faits et Chiffres, q.v.

'Unemployed Youth: an African Symposium', *International Labour Review*, Vol. LXXXVII, No. 3, March 1963.

'Youth Employment and Vocational Training Schemes in the Developing Countries', ibid., Vol. LXXXVI, No. 3, September 1962.

CHAPTER 7

Notes

(1) Colin Legum: *Bandung, Cairo and Accra*, London, the Africa Bureau, 1958, p. 5.

(2) See Colin Legum: *Pan-Africanism: a short political guide*, London and Dunmow, Pall Mall Press, 1962, p. 230.

(3) Quoted in Colin Legum: *Congo Disaster*, London, Penguin Books, 1961, p. 153. The full text may be found in U.N. Document A/4711, Addendum 2.

(4) See Legum: *Pan-Africanism*, p. 177.

(5) Quoted in L. Hamon: 'Le Parti fédérale africain et le Rassemblement démocratique africain de la querelle fédéraliste à l'indépendance (1959–1960). II. le R.D.A.', q.v., p. 350.

(6) L. S. Senghor: 'Rapport sur la Doctrine et le Programme du Parti', q.v.

(7) Legum: *Pan-Africanism*, p. 198.

(8) Quoted by Legum, ibid., p. 174.

(9) See Legum, ibid., p. 54.

(10) *Chronologie politique africaine*, second year, No. 6, November–December 1961, p. 12.

(11) See Kwame Nkrumah: *Africa Must Unite*, q.v., p. 197.

(12) *Chronologie politique africaine*, second year, No. 4, July–August 1961, p. 57.

(13) ibid., fourth year, No. 1, January–February 1963, pp. 20-1.

(14) Quoted in *West Africa*, 1 June 1963.

Some Additional Reading

American Society of African Culture (edit.): *Pan-Africanism Reconsidered*, Berkeley and Los Angeles, University of California Press, 1962.

Austin, Dennis: 'The Uncertain Frontier: Ghana–Togo', *The Journal of Modern African Studies*, Vol. I, No. 2, June 1963.

Carter, Gwendolen M. (edit.): *African One-Party States*, q.v.

Cohen, Sir Andrew: 'The New Africa and the United Nations', in *Africa: A Handbook to the Continent*, edited by Colin Legum, London, Anthony Blond, 1961.

Cowan, L. Gray: 'Nigerian Foreign Policy', *The Nigerian Political Scene*, q.v.

Decraene, Philippe: *Le Panafricanisme*, Paris, Presses Universitaires de France, 1959.

Dia, Mamadou: *The African Nations and World Solidarity*, q.v.

Du Bois, Victor D.: 'Changing Relations among Guinea, the Ivory Coast and Mali', American Universities Field Staff Reports Service, West Africa Series, Vol. V, No. 4.

Good, Robert C.: 'Congo Crisis: the Role of the New States', in *Neutralism*, edited by Arnold Wolfers, Washington D.C., Center of Foreign Policy Research, 1961.

Helleiner, Gerald K.: 'Nigeria and the African Common Market', the *Nigerian Journal of Economic and Social Studies*, Vol. 4, No. 3, November 1962.

Hoskyns, Catherine: *The Congo: a Chronology of Events, January 1960–December 1961*, London, Oxford University Press for the Royal Institute of International Affairs, May 1962, mimeographed.

Hovet, T.: *Africa in the United Nations*, Evanston, Northwestern University Press, 1963.

Lorch, Netanel: 'Israel and Africa', *The World Today*, Vol. 19, No. 8, August 1963.

McKay, Vernon: *Africa in World Politics*, New York and Evanston, Harper and Row, 1963.

Padelford, Norman J., and Emerson, Rupert (edit.): *Africa and World Order*, New York, Frederick A. Praeger, 1963.

Padmore, George: *Pan-Africanism or Communism? The Coming Struggle for Africa*, London, Dennis Dobson, 1956.

Rivkin, Arnold: *Africa and the West*, London, Thames and Hudson, 1962.

Thiam, Doudou: *La Politique étrangère des États africains*, Paris, Presses Universitaires de France, 1963.

Wallerstein, Immanuel: *Africa: the Politics of Independence*, q.v.

'Africa's Future: the Soviet View', supplement to *MIZAN Newsletter*, No. 4, April 1961. (An abridged translation of I. Potekhin's 'Afrika Smotrit v Budushcheye'.)

CHAPTER 8

Notes

(1) *Afrique Nouvelle*, No. 828, 21–7 June, 1963.
(2) *Congo Disaster*, q.v., p. 145.
(3) See a report in *Afrique Nouvelle*, No. 820, 26 April–2 May 1963.

Index